THE
COLLEGE INSTRUCTOR'S
GUIDE TO
TEACHING AND
ACADEMIA

Roy Udolf

THE COLLEGE INSTRUCTOR'S GUIDE TO TEACHING AND ACADEMIA

Nelson-Hall nh Chicago

LIBRARY OF CONGRESS CATALOGING IN PUBLICATION DATA

Udolf, Roy.
    The college instructor's guide to teaching and
academia.

    Includes index.
        1.   College teaching—Handbooks, manuals, etc.
I.   Title.
LB2331.U3   378.1'2   76–7462
ISBN 0–88229–241–2

Copyright © 1976 by Roy Udolf

Manufactured in the United States of America

To Marcelle who never complained when I left a respectable job to pursue a hobby.

Contents

Acknowledgments

I am indebted to the following people for their substantial assistance in the preparation of this book. . . . They are in no way to be deemed responsible either for the opinions expressed or for any remaining errors contained herein.

Ms. Emily Sillman who typed the entire manuscript.

Professors Alfred Cohn, Ira Rubin, and Shirley Langer who reviewed the manuscript and made many helpful suggestions.

David Udolf who graciously provided me with enough release time from my responsibilities as a father to complete this book.

Preface

To the young person beginning an academic career the first class of his own can be both an exciting opportunity and a nightmare.

He may bring an impressive set of academic credentials in his area of specialization to this class, but he is about to be called upon to do work with it that he has received no training for at all. If he is not fortunate enough to have a more experienced colleague who is willing to take the time to guide him through an inevitable series of early trials, he is likely either to decide that college teaching isn't for him and leave teaching or to settle down into the pattern of habitual, mediocre performance that is all too common on college campuses.

The specific goal of this book is to provide a guide for the beginning college instructor and to help him cope with the many problems that will surely beset him in his early (and later) years in academia.

This book attempts to be more than just a how-to-do-it manual of useful teaching techniques and ideas. It tries to prepare the neophyte professor for handling problems with colleagues, campus politics, and the administration as well as with students. It should also give a person considering an academic career an accurate idea of what college teaching is like and provide a realistic basis upon which to decide if it's the type of work to which he would want to commit the rest of his life.

While intended primarily for beginning college instructors or graduate students preparing for their first teaching assignment, this book hopefully provides some ideas worth considering even for more experienced faculty and for educators other than college teachers. There is much in this book with which the more experienced teacher will agree and possibly some things with which he will violently disagree.

No book by itself can make a great teacher out of the reader. I will be well satisfied if this book helps to make the reader's early years in academia as trauma free as possible and aids him in attaining his full potential as a teacher.

1.
Is College Teaching for You?

If you are not a friend or relative of mine and you've just bought a copy of this book, then it's a fairly reasonable assumption that you are interested in a career in college teaching. Before going any further what you need is a candid appraisal of both the rewards and the drawbacks of an academic career. This will give you some basis for making an informed decision as to whether or not you would like to spend the rest of your life doing this type of work. The average person works eight hours a day, five days a week for over forty years. To be trapped for this period of time in a job that yields no satisfaction beyond a periodic paycheck represents a tragic destruction of a human life. In the case of a teacher this tragedy is multiplied many thousandfold because of the great potential influence, for good or ill, that a teacher has on the lives of his students. It is true that a college professor does not deal with students quite as plastic as those dealt with in grade schools (where incompetent teachers should be executed, not fired, to assure that they stay out of teaching). Nevertheless an incompetent or inept college teacher is such a potentially destructive influence on students that he is a menace that no university can afford in spite of his ubiquitous presence on

1

college campuses. This is true no matter how eminent he may be in other fields such as research, or how extensively he has published.

What will be considered in this chapter, therefore, are the rewards and penalties of a college teaching career and the professional and personal qualifications of a successful teacher.

On the positive side of the ledger there are many attractive aspects to teaching. For one thing, in most universities there is true professional status in the sense that you come and go as you please and can usually arrange your working hours in accordance with your personal preferences. This is a different situation from that found in industry where practically everyone from the corporation president on down punches a time clock, at least figuratively.

A full-time teaching load ranges from nine to twelve hours exclusive of required office hours. The balance of your time will be taken up with committee activities, preparing for courses, grading papers, talking to students and colleagues, and furthering your own education.

To a large extent you are your own boss and in a well run department no one will tell you what to include in your lectures or how to deliver them, although many beginning instructors may often wish someone would.

Your colleagues will be highly trained professional people and an academic department can provide an intellectually stimulating atmosphere at times.

On the other hand, while in some respects you are your own boss, in a real sense an academic department is run more by committees than by the nominal chairman. This is especially true if the chairman is an ineffective leader or a poor manager, and most academicians have little training or skill in these areas. As a result of this type of collective management many departments are wracked by internal political factions, and not only can this destroy the effectiveness of the department but it can constitute a serious impediment to the individual work of a professor. Thus, a professor may discover that in such important matters as salary, promotion, and tenure he has not one but dozens of bosses to please, and this is a totally untenable position. Especially if, as is often the case, the members of the committees themselves are unable to agree as to what the standards for promotion or tenure should be.

There are other drawbacks to academia, not the least of which is financial. In American society social position and status are directly related to income. For the degree of training and education required of a college professor, salaries are unbelievably low. Furthermore, this situation is likely to get even worse before it gets better as colleges are cranking out Ph.D.'s today at a rate far in excess of any reasonable employment prospects for these graduates. This is probably due to the middle-class obsession with education as a status symbol and the general idea that education somehow is the panacea for all human problems.

For a young person starting out in life, salaries may not be too horrendous, but if you have the idea of changing fields later in life (and for some reason many people dream of teaching when they retire), it will be almost impossible to ever catch up to where you were financially or even to survive without relying on outside consulting work.

It may seem strange that in a society so obsessed with education college professors are accorded so little status, but this is probably the result of the raising of the educational level, or at least the number of years of formal schooling, of the average American, who is no longer awed by academic degrees. Whatever the reason, the days are long since past when college professors were placed on pedestals and regarded as infallible. While those of us in the field may be a little chagrined at this development, it is probably a healthy thing, for few people have the strength of character to withstand being treated like a quasi-deity without suffering serious damage to their professional and personal integrity.

As an example of the real status of a college teacher, the City of New York pays its garbage collectors more than many colleges pay their faculty. At least one person has suggested to me that this was because garbage collectors were more important to society than college professors. In many respects they undoubtedly are. It is not possible for a society to survive without garbage collectors while it can survive without professors. It can also survive without music, art, or literature. The real question is whether there would really be any point to a mere physical survival without any of these uniquely human activities.

If your prime interest is to attain a high status in life or even to provide a decent standard of living for your family, don't consider college teaching. It's hard to imagine any other area of human activity requiring the same amount of training that teaching does where you can't do substantially better on both counts.

While the status of a professor with the public at large may have deteriorated over the years, what is harder for the beginning teacher whose prime interest is in teaching to accept is the fact that colleges are not designed either for teachers or students. In spite of the lip service given to such terms as "quality teaching" or "innovative teaching," teaching ability still remains one of the least highly regarded attributes of a faculty member and is thus the least highly rewarded. Indeed the professor's advancement in rank and salary and his attaining tenure will be much more dependent on how much he has published or on his political skills than on his basic worth as a teacher. This is the reason why college faculties are loaded down with insensitive, inept, and downright incompetent "teachers" to an extent far beyond what would be predicted from the normal distribution of human abilities. This is also the reason why you may have noticed that there are no famous teachers. Certainly there are many famous people who incidentally teach, but none of these are famous for their teaching activities. Indeed we are probably the only profession in the world that is not deemed important enough to produce celebrities.

There are many reasons set forth for the current emphasis on research and publication on college campuses. One such argument is that by publication the university acquires a national reputation and can draw upon the entire population of the country for potential students. It is of course highly desirable to have a diverse student body as students learn at least as much from each other as from the faculty. However, in over ten years of college teaching I have never met a student who came to his school because of reading an article by a faculty member.

Another argument often heard is that true scholarship involves advancing human knowledge and universities should be in the forefront of this advance. More will be said about this in Chapter 13, "Publish or Perish."

The young instructor soon discovers real pressures to do research and publish, and he may begin to doubt whether teaching in its own right is really a worthwhile or at least a respectable vocation. If you don't have a strong conviction that it is, you will probably be unable to withstand these pressures and, like many others, you may be converted from a possibly talented teacher to a third rate academic hack writer.

This is not to deny that there is a real need for people in research. If it wasn't for these people, teachers wouldn't have much material to organize and explain to their classes. Furthermore, there is no reason why a teacher shouldn't get involved with research if he is interested in it and doesn't unduly neglect his students. However, it is a totally different field of endeavor than teaching and is by no means a necessary prerequisite for effective college teaching. It is a rare person indeed who is equally talented in both areas. In fact, it is a rare person who is talented in either area.

While I recognize a real need for researchers I am not so convinced that their place is in a university as opposed to a research organization. However, a convincing argument can be made for the presence of research oriented people on college faculties, to some degree. Even if you believe that the primary function of a university is to educate students, an education consists of exposing the student to a variety of different ideas, and you can't have a diversity of ideas without having a diverse faculty. The real objection to the emphasis on research on college campuses is the resultant downgrading of teaching skills that it tends to produce. People, like rats, learn to do what they are reinforced for doing.

Nobody in a university, of course, will ever say that quality teaching or students aren't important, any more than they would come out in favor of ethnic discrimination or venereal disease. What they will say instead are such things as "We're all good teachers but we have to do something more." I doubt that any student in America would be prepared to agree with such a statement concerning the faculty at his institution.

There are a few rare and gifted individuals who are talented both as teachers and researchers. I have been fortunate enough to know a few of them. However, there aren't enough such people to fill any significant portion of the faculty positions on American campuses. Since there aren't enough of these people to populate our college faculties, an election must be made between research oriented and student oriented faculty. It is my personal belief that both types ought to be represented on a balanced faculty, but that the balance should be heavier in the area of teaching because the prime responsibility of a college is the education and development of its students.

While there is a great overproduction of Ph.D.'s and faculty positions are hard to find, there is actually a severe shortage of first rate teachers, just as there is a severe shortage of first rate doctors, lawyers, mechanics or top people in any line of work. Fortunately, there are many excellent books available to teach the mechanics of quality research. Unfortunately, however, there are none available to teach how to develop the creativity necessary to do this. This book is designed to teach the mechanical aspects underlying quality teaching.

Perhaps the most important advantage to a career in college teaching is that every term the university will provide you free of charge a new group of students with whom to work. In the last analysis your students will provide you with all of the reinforcement for your efforts in preparing and conducting your classes. They will supply you with enough problems to prevent your professional life from ever becoming dull. They will also keep you honest by giving you lots of adverse stimulation when you do an inferior job.

To a large extent how much you enjoy teaching is a function of your interactions with your students and how sensitive you are to their needs, interests, and responses. If you don't enjoy working with all of them, not just the occasional genius, if you're not positively or negatively reinforced by their responses to your lectures, you would do both yourself and your students a favor by going into some other line of work. Teaching will hold few rewards and innumerable vexations for you. If you do enjoy working with all types of students, they will make all of the drawbacks of academia seem trivial and you will find teaching a richly satisfying career at least in nonfinancial terms.

If after considering the pro's and con's of college teaching carefully, you believe you could be happy and successful at it, the next thing to consider is what personal and professional qualifications are necessary. In most fields a Ph.D. will ultimately be required even though there are teaching positions that you can obtain while working toward this degree. In some professional fields like law or medicine different terminal degrees are required, but in general you will need the highest degree offered in your field for a permanent teaching career.

Besides having a terminal degree, in order to teach any course effectively you have to be an expert in the course area. This does not mean that you have to know everything about the subject. Some people think that they do but they are wrong; nobody does. As a good working definition, an expert is one who knows at least twenty times more about his subject than his students do. Obviously there will be some areas in your general field that you know less about than others. If you are called upon to teach a course in such an area, the first problem you will have is becoming an expert in a short period of time. This essentially involves utilizing your skills as a student. One of the most basic requirements of being a good teacher is therefore to be a top flight student. As long as you stay in teaching, you are going to be first and foremost a student, if for no other reason than to keep your grasp of your field current.

Besides being an expert in your own field a broad general education in many other areas is an indispensable asset to a teacher. It permits you to see and point up relationships between principles in your field and others and helps your students develop new insights and a broader perspective. No narrow expert in the accommodation reflex in albino rats will ever become a great teacher, because he lacks the broad range of interests which is so essential in exciting interest in his students.

Even more important than the professional qualifications of a teacher are his personal qualifications. Teaching involves the interaction between a professor and his students, and unless he has the type of personality that enjoys this type of interaction and the social situation involved in the classroom he will never enjoy his work and therefore his students won't either. Nothing will destroy student interest more quickly than to have to sit through a lecture given by someone who would obviously rather be somewhere else. Teaching is really a form of show business, and a successful teacher like a successful performer needs an outgoing type of personality.

Besides being a showman a teacher also occupies a leadership role with his class, and it's hard to be an effective teacher without having some leadership ability. Things that tend to make for poor quality leadership such as pomposity, being overimpressed with your own importance or being unconcerned with the needs of your group also make for a poor quality of teacher-student relationships. A successful teacher is primarily concerned with the progress and general welfare of his students. This is because the only real satisfaction in a teacher's work is the result of the accomplishments of his students. When a student flunks a course or does more poorly in it than his ability would predict, in a real sense the professor has also failed.

Like the reader, I have had an occasional great teacher during my own student days, several abominable ones, and a host of mediocre ones. It is one of the basic purposes of this book to point up what the differences between great and substandard teachers are. The question often arises, are great teachers made or born? Can you really learn to be a first rate teacher? Probably the answer is that everybody has a certain degree of potential for any type of work, and training can maximize whatever talent you bring into the field.

I suspect that if there is any common denominator to success in different fields of human endeavor, it is the ability to enjoy what you are doing and to get reinforced by the feeling that you've done a good job. Clearly this is true in teaching, for if you enjoy a course your students will, and when they enjoy it they will learn more. If you don't they won't; it's as simple as that. Thus, a good teacher has to be sensitive enough to respond to student reactions. If you've just given a lecture and you have the feeling that it was terrible, that is a good sign. It shows that you have this basic sensitivity and are thus capable of becoming a first rate teacher. It's only when you don't recognize when you've done a poor job or don't care that you are hopeless.

There are other attributes that are nice for a professor to have, like being independently wealthy or having a spouse with a good job, but these are not really essential. Teaching can be such a fun type of job for the right person that if you think you might like it, you owe it to yourself to give it a try. If you are right for this work you will find yourself looking forward to meeting with your classes each day and resenting it when classes are called off during snowstorms or holidays.

2.
The Goals of College Teaching

It is always helpful to have a clear idea of what you are attempting to do. Therefore, at the onset a teacher should have general and specific goals both to know what he is working toward and to be able to accurately gauge his success or failure. Certain teaching goals may be called general because they apply to every course you will ever teach and some, for a particular course or even for a particular class or student, may be classified as specific.

Your goals must be realistic. They must be attainable, unless you are a masochist who enjoys going through life constantly failing. On the other hand, they must be challenging enough to demand that you produce the maximum that you are capable of if you are to attain any real satisfaction in reaching these goals. In order to be able to set realistic goals for yourself there are certain basic ideas that you need concerning what a teacher really is and what he actually does.

The word "teacher" is one of the grossest misnomers in the English language. In fact, no teacher ever teaches anyone anything. Every first-year graduate student in psychology knows that learning is an active process and that each of us must do his own. Think of it for a minute. The greatest

11

teacher who ever lived couldn't teach a goldfish how to swim!

If he doesn't teach anything, then what does a teacher do? Is he really some kind of fraud taking money under false pretenses? Not necessarily. What a good teacher actually does is to facilitate the student's learning process. He does this in a variety of ways.

If he's really good, he arouses the student's interest in the material. This permits the student to pay attention for a longer time span with less effort and takes much of the onus out of his studies. Transforming study from a work to a recreational activity is the mark of a truly great teacher. Psychologists call this process motivating a student, and it is a major goal of all teachers.

Another thing that an effective teacher does is to organize the material in a course in such a way as to make it easier for the student to master principles and relationships as well as isolated facts.

A good teacher ties things together and points up relationships; a great teacher leads his students to the point where they will discover these relationships for themselves. This is, of course, vastly more satisfying to the student than being spoonfed, for then his discovery is his own, not the instructor's; he gets not just the insight but the thrill of personal discovery.

A third way that an instructor can help a student learn is by interacting with him. More than just answering questions clearly when they arise, important as this may be, interacting means that during a lecture the student plays an active role —he thinks and responds rather than sits passively as he is being talked at. It also includes informal conversations with students outside of class. These are often more effective than lectures in driving home a point because they are more personal and the student is more actively involved. There is much psychological evidence that the more active the learning process the better the retention.

From the foregoing you can see that two general goals of any teacher are:

1. To arouse student interest and motivation.
2. To assist the student in his learning efforts by facilitating his work.

In view of these general goals it is hard to understand why many instructors inflict such a variety of aversive tasks on their students. These have the general effect of making the course a succession of obstacles and turning students off. Examples of these senseless tasks would include such things as:

—Requiring constant trips to a library when suitable material is available in a text or readings book.

—Giving reading lists which include references of questionable quality or contain items of little value in relationship to the study time they require.

—Assigning reports, term papers, or problems without making a careful appraisal of their educational value to the student in relation to the amount of time that they require of him.

The prime function of a teacher is to help a student, not to waste his time. Students need a reasonable amount of time to read their texts, rework their notes, or just think about the course. It has been argued that many students if not given specific assignments will not do work on their own, and of course this is true. However, those students who would work independently ought to be given the opportunity to do so.

The function of a teacher is not to force an unwilling student to work. Motivating the student is his function. College students are either adults or in the process of becoming adults and ought to be treated as such. How much or how little a student chooses to get out of your course is basically his own business. If you have the desire to force people to do things you would be happier working in a prison rather than in a college.

Do not jump to the inaccurate conclusion that I am opposed to assignments or term papers *in a proper case.* My point is that anything you assign should be designed to achieve some specific purpose worth the time that you're requiring your students to invest. Busy work and excessive assignments are the hallmark of an incompetent teacher.

Beyond the general goals of teaching each course will involve a set of more specific goals such as the mastery of certain important facts, relationships, skills and ideas. Your first step in preparing an outline for a new course should be listing these specific goals. Two competent professors teaching the same course may differ sharply over the important specific goals they list, but no one should ever be entrusted with a class who can't verbalize his own specific goals clearly and in detail.

Even graduate classes tend to be heterogeneous in terms of student interests and abilities, and it is not realistic to expect all students to come away from the course with the same increment in learning. Nor is this necessarily desirable. However, minimum course goals can be established.

Beyond the general and specific goals that the instructor sets for himself he ought to have some philosophy of the overall goals of the educational process. Some people feel that the goals of education are to acquire a collection of facts and relationships or some degree of vocational skill. Others talk vaguely about such concepts as "learning to think" or "learning how to do research or find answers."

I do not think that education is synonymous with vocational training, whether as a mechanic or a researcher. If, on the other hand, education consisted of learning a collection of facts and theories, it would be a futile endeavor, because the student who doesn't actually use this material daily will forget the bulk of it within months after graduation.

It appears to me that the essence of the educational process is the exposure of the student to a variety of ideas which he is free to mull over and think about and which he selectively and tentatively accepts or rejects. This occurs in a more concentrated manner during the college years but it is a process which continues throughout life. Indeed this is one of the unique features of human beings, and it is hard to conceive of a person who is never exposed to new facts and ideas as being intellectually alive.

If education consists of exposure to new ideas then obviously one of the goals of any teacher must be to include enough important and relevant ideas in his course to give his students an adequate exposure to the area defined by the course title. Furthermore, these ideas along with their current status must be presented clearly and interestingly, and evaluative opinions concerning them, including the instructor's own, must be given.

In effect, universities, like shoe factories, produce a product. Our product is an educated student. Not a skilled craftsman, not an expert in using a library, not a walking collection of information, but a person who has been exposed to a variety of ideas and opinions and has developed his own frame of reference by which to evaluate them—an activity which he will engage in for the rest of his life.

As previously stated, goals to be useful must be realistic. What you can accomplish realistically with a class is a function of a particular class as well as your own abilities and limitations. With experience you will learn to make more accurate estimates of what you can and cannot achieve.

One of the dangers of talking to your colleagues about course goals (unless you know them really well) is that you both begin talking in terms of socially acceptable goals that may sound good at department meetings but which have no counterpart in reality. For example, I have heard people describe in detail all of the specific skills that their students were going to take away from an introductory psychological statistics course. This sounded impressive, but professors who have been around psychology students long enough know that they, like engineering students, begin to learn math in their experimental courses when they are first called upon to utilize these techniques in the solution of practical problems.

Thus, my major goals for an introductory course in statistics are:

1. To change the student's original negative attitude toward the subject.
2. To lay a sound foundation to facilitate the future learning of specific techniques in subsequent courses.

These goals don't sound as impressive as to expect students to be able to do a split plot analysis of variance, but they are more realistic.

Professors, like students, ought to learn from each course that they teach, and course goals ought to be continuously modified to reflect this learning. Unrealistic goals must be modified and made attainable; goals that are too easy to attain must be upgraded or supplemented so that you have to extend yourself to attain them.

A set of worthy and realistic goals will provide you with direction in your work. They are merely a starting point, but without them you are assured of failure.

3.

Becoming and Remaining an Expert in Your Field

The question is often asked, why should a Ph.D. or other terminal degree be required for a professor? The best teacher in a department may be one with a master's degree. Also, there are enough abominable teachers having Ph.D.'s to prove to the most skeptical that this degree is in no way an index of teaching ability. I suspect that if there is any justification for this requirement it is that the degree is some evidence of ability as a student. This skill is vital, for as long as you are going to remain in teaching you must first and foremost be a student.

By the time the newly minted doctor of philosophy frames his diploma he's already on his way to becoming obsolete and only a lifetime of effort can prevent or at least slow down this process. In many fields of learning the explosion of new knowledge and theories is so rapid that no one can be knowledgeable about the entire field. Some formal plan of continuing education will be necessary just to keep generally informed about the entire field and to remain up to date in your special areas. A Ph.D. may be a terminal degree in the sense that it is the highest offered in a field, but it is by no means the end of an education; it is really just the beginning.

No matter how well trained a person may be there will always be vastly more that he is ignorant of than knowledgeable about in his field. There are two major types of ignorance. One type is where the ignorance is universally shared and the other is where the ignorance is merely personal. Knowledge of the former material is gained through original research and experimentation; knowledge of the latter is attained through library research, seminars, and the like. Both types of research appear to be equally respectable and productive to me. Both may result in publishable works and both are incapable of completion during a human life span. The average college professor will be involved to some degree with both types of research during his career but probably more of the latter since it is a prerequisite to doing original research as well as a necessary preliminary step in course preparation.

What is about to be discussed now are some of the methods of alleviating personal ignorance and keeping professional knowledge updated. The peculiar advantages and disadvantages associated with each of these methods will also be considered. The reader will ultimately have to decide which combination and what proportion of these techniques will best serve his personal situation, taking into account his field of specialization, professional commitments, and available time. Some formal plan of continuing education, however, is an absolutely essential professional obligation. This is too important a matter to be left to happenstance, as a professor's courses can never be any better than the state of his professional knowledge.

SEMINARS AND FORMAL COURSES

There are usually a number of seminars and lectures available in most large population centers that can be profitable. They may be single lectures by eminent people in the field or a series of lectures. These are usually sponsored by professional societies or universities. Larger universities often offer formal postdoctoral programs leading to certificates of completion, which seems to me to be contrary to the whole concept of education as a lifelong process. This, however, doesn't detract from the substantive value of these programs.

Another source of formal course work is, of course, regular university programs. There is no law against taking a course that you are interested in or in need of after you graduate. As a matter of fact it is not impossible for a Ph.D. to learn a lot even from an undergraduate course. For one thing he may get some fresh ideas in teaching from seeing how others approach the material. Taking courses outside of your own field or even taking a degree in another subject can give you new insights and broaden your base of knowledge.

Formal courses and lectures have many advantages. For one thing they tend to be an efficient way of being exposed to a lot of material in a short period of time. Also they require regular learning habits, which are useful if you have a tendency to put things off. If you are careful to seek out courses with different people, you will find much material that you can incorporate into your own lectures to improve them. The major drawback to this method of keeping current is that it can become expensive. However, the expense can be reduced considerably by asking permission to sit in on courses. If the course is not part of a formal postdoctoral program most professors will be flattered to have a colleague wanting to sit in on their courses and will readily grant such a request.

PROFESSIONAL MEETINGS

The average college professor will probably belong to several professional societies that hold annual conventions. These provide an opportunity to meet with and talk to colleagues from all over the country and to attend a variety of seminars or to give one. The attending of one or two conventions a year is an excellent idea but can become a major expense even if tax deductible. This is especially true if your spouse decides to have you combine business with a short vacation and comes along. One way of reducing this expense is to limit your attendance to nearby conventions. Another technique is to present a paper or to preside over a seminar yourself, as many colleges will reimburse part of your expenses in attending a convention only if you are on the program. Attendance at a convention will also give you an idea of what job opportunities are currently available in different parts of the country.

PROFESSIONAL JOURNALS

All professional societies publish journals, and membership in most societies will result in your receiving a number of journals regularly. Other journals in your field will be available in the library.

Journals should be scanned regularly for material of interest. If the journal requires abstracts of its authors, as many do, these can be useful in letting you know if the article is worth your time to read. Journals, however, suffer from two important drawbacks as a method of keeping current. Due to the inane publish or perish policies of many universities there is a deluge of articles appearing that should never have been written, and these articles tend to bury the few good ones.

Secondly, due to the same deluge of articles submitted for publication many journals have substantial publication lags. The "latest" article that you are reading may describe an experiment run several years ago.

If you are researching a specific problem or preparing a new course then you would naturally not rely on scanning the latest issues of professional journals but would undertake a more formal search for relevant material, utilizing the appropriate abstracts for the last five or ten years. Each article you find in the abstracts will have its own reference section and this will lead you into a chain of relevant material. It will also give you an idea of the people who are working in this area.

TEXTS AND BOOKS

College professors are inundated with sample textbooks submitted by publishers for possible use in college courses. In the course of their evaluation of these books professors are incidentally exposed to current material as textbooks tend to be constantly updated.

If you desire a book primarily for your own use, then propriety requires that you buy it rather than request an examination copy, but most publishers and college bookstores will afford you a professional discount. Even with this discount, books tend to be expensive both financially and in terms of time, so it will pay you to be selective.

If you choose carefully you will find that a planned program of reading is also an efficient way of keeping current. You can do a lot of reading at no expense by utilizing your school library, but it has been my experience that if a book is worth reading it is worth owning for future reference. Perhaps the best plan is to read it first and if it proves worthwhile, order a copy for your own library.

DISCUSSIONS WITH COLLEAGUES

A well-constituted academic department will contain a diversity of expertise in many different subspecialities of your field. Our students learn a great deal from us and it is somewhat ludicrous that we often do not take the opportunity to learn from each other. Few departments have formal programs of faculty education, but despite this deplorable fact we can learn a great deal informally.

Often a question or two asked of a colleague will save hours of library research. The reason that many professors do not take advantage of this source of information is probably that they are reluctant to admit that there is anything about their field that they do not know. This is a maladaptive symptom of insecurity that it would be well to outgrow.

For example, I have been the beneficiary of extensive amounts of free consulting services for my vegetable garden as the result of simply asking questions of a plant expert in the neighboring biology department.

Discussions with colleagues will often provide you with new insights into old ideas and can often help to crystallize your own thinking.

INTERACTION WITH STUDENTS

It may seem a little odd to talk about learning from students when your prime responsibility is in educating them, but, nevertheless, a major portion of your continuing education will come from your students. One major impetus to this process will be the questions that they ask and you can't answer. Incidentally, the best approach to this situation is to frankly admit that you don't know the answer and undertake to find it out. If your pride causes you to try to bluff your way out you will convert a perfectly normal situation into an embarrassing one that stands a good chance of destroying your rapport with an entire class. The odds are that you won't get away with this deception. Students, in general, are quite sharp and no one has much respect for a phony. Not knowing the answers to student questions is a reasonably common occurrence and is a good sign that your students are being stimulated to thought. This is one of the few times that a student gets the chance to give an instructor an assignment. Never ask the student to look up and report on the answer unless you are trying to stifle all future questions.

No matter how long you have been teaching it will never cease to amaze you how often students will give you new insights or suggest problems that you've never thought about.

Often the process of preparing or revising lectures will have the same effect.

If you think about it for a minute you will realize that every student, even in an elementary course, knows some things that the instructor doesn't, especially in areas peripheral to the course. It is an inept and insensitive instructor who doesn't learn a great deal from his students. This is particularly true in advanced or graduate courses or in evening courses where the majority of the students may be adults representing a wide range of vocational experience.

If you find that you don't learn much from your students it probably means that you're talking at them rather than communicating with them, and this is a major fault requiring correction.

4.

Interaction with Students

The major portion of a professor's work involves interacting in some manner with his students. This interaction may occur in a variety of settings. It may be on a group basis in the classroom or at college functions, or it may occur on an individual basis in the instructor's office or more informally in the cafeteria or on the campus.

This chapter is concerned with the more personal one-to-one situations. These situations can be further subdivided into formal business meetings where the objective is quite specific and the less formal, general social situations.

In the formal situation the student has either made an appointment to see you or has dropped around during your office hours with some specific problem. This problem may involve his understanding of some aspect of your course, his concern over his grades, his seeking guidance in planning a program, or getting into a graduate school or less specifically, his planning for future vocational goals.

Sometimes you will have initiated the interview as, for example, if you are concerned about the student's course performance.

Aside from these purely professional problems, students bring personal and emotional problems to faculty members with whom they have developed a personal relationship and in whom they have confidence. These are often less clearly verbalized and are harder to deal with than the professional problems unless the faculty member happens to be a psychologist or is trained in some allied discipline.

There are some general principles that will aid you in dealing with student problems:

1. Before doing anything else listen carefully to what the student says and then question him until you are sure that you understand exactly what his problem is.

2. You may wish to share your own experiences, but do not undertake to solve personal or emotional problems that require special training unless you have such training. Rather you should be familiar with those local or campus organizations to which the student can be referred to get the skilled professional help he needs.

3. After understanding the problem and deciding that it's within your professional scope, give specific advice. Don't tell a student to work harder who claims to be working four hours a day on a course that he's flunking. Try to find out exactly what he's doing wrong and point out to him what he should try instead. This type of advice takes more time to give than general statements extolling the virtues of hard work and motherhood, but it is the only way in which you can be effective. If you are not enough of a student to recognize ineffective versus effective methods of study in a particular course, you shouldn't be teaching in the first place.

4. Follow up on your advice. Arrange for a subsequent meeting to find out if the problem has been helped or if it requires that some other alternatives be tried.

With respect to graduate or professional school admissions

you ought to have a good knowledge about what the various schools require in the way of preparation and grades and also what other factors they look for in candidates for admission. The medical and law schools have organizations that publish catalogues listing this information for all medical and law schools for the guidance of potential candidates. Most professional societies publish similar summaries of graduate school data such as the American Psychological Association's catalogue on graduate study in psychology. You ought to have current copies of these in your office. It will not be practical for you to collect bulletins from all of the individual graduate schools but your college library should have them available.

The student who knows what graduate program he is interested in getting into is much less of a problem than the student who doesn't really know what he wants to do and comes to you seeking guidance. No matter what your academic specialty, as long as you remain on a college campus you are going to find yourself in the role of a vocational counselor whether you like it or not. This requires that you be aware of graduate programs in many fields other than your own and of the major professional programs as well. This knowledge should include as a minimum, admission requirements to these programs and some of the major vocational opportunities and drawbacks in these fields so that you can inform your advisees in some detail.

Giving vocational advice to students requires that the interests and abilities of the individual student be considered. At no time should you ever tell a student that he should or shouldn't enter a particular program. What you ought to do is provide him with enough information so that he is able to make an intelligent choice. The more information you have concerning the alternatives open to the student the better will be the quality of the advice that you can give him. There will be times when neither you nor the student knows enough about the student's interests and abilities to make an intelligent decision. In such a case you might refer him to the college guidance office for interest and ability testing if your school has such a facility. If a guidance office is lacking, one should be organized.

The most common situation in which a student seeks guidance is in program planning. In most colleges he is assigned an advisor who must approve his program and sign his registration card each term. Thus, this type of consultation occurs mostly around registration time.

Often students will come around and say that they have to register today and they can't find their advisor, so would you please sign their program card for them. This practice will ultimately undermine the entire concept of student advisement and eventually will do great harm to the students using it. If you do sign a student's program card you have an obligation to question him and check out the suitability of the courses that he wants to take. He should also be told to inform his regular advisor of this program.

Planning student programs requires that you be familiar with all of the requirements for graduation both of your college and your department. If your department doesn't have one then you ought to make yourself a set of mimeographed requirement sheets that you can use as a worksheet for each of your advisees. This will enable you to keep track of what he has taken and is taking and to be sure that he will graduate on schedule. It is also a good idea to record on this sheet each time that a student comes to you for program planning. It is useful to know that the advisee complaining that he wasn't properly advised and therefore won't graduate on time never came in to seek advice. Figure 1 in the appendix is an example of such a form.

Another common office visit involves the student's seeking a letter of recommendation for a graduate school or a potential employer. Sometimes students will request these by leaving you a note. In all cases the student ought to be contacted so that you can get all of the information that you will need most expeditiously. To write an effective recommendation you will need to know at least the following:

1. To whom is the recommendation to be sent and when is it required to be submitted
2. How long have you known the student and in what capacity, e.g., student, advisee, assistant, departmental assistant
3. How well do you know him
4. What courses did he take with you and what were his grades
5. When did he take these courses (so that you can check on the accuracy of his statements)
6. What is his grade point average overall and in his major
7. What honorary societies is he a member of and what prizes and awards has he received
8. In what extracurricular activities has he participated
9. What is his work experience, if any
10. What else does he think you should know about him before writing your recommendation.

If you undertake to write a letter of recommendation on behalf of a student then you have committed yourself to helping him to get into a program. The letter ought to be as positive as possible consistent with being honest. If you don't feel that you can say anything positive about the student then you ought to explain to the student what you would have to write and see if he prefers that you decline to write a recommendation.

You owe it to your own reputation to make letters of recommendation as accurate as possible. If you habitually write extravagant letters of praise every time you are asked to write a reference, in a short period of time this will be recognized and your letters on behalf of the most deserving candidates will carry little or no weight.

Often you will be asked to write a letter on behalf of a

student of whom you know nothing adverse, but whom you don't know well enough to be able to say anything positive either. In such a case you would do well to tell the candidate of this and suggest that he ask some faculty member who knows him better to write. Sometimes, as in the case of a student returning to school after a number of years' absence, there may be no faculty member around who really knows him well enough. In this case you will have to do the best you can with whatever information you can dig up. You should candidly advise the student of just how good a recommendation you are in a position to give him. For the sake of your own reputation, student information should be checked for accuracy. Opinions that you have that are not based on personal knowledge should be so labeled.

Many departments have developed check off forms with space for additional comments that can be used instead of letters of recommendation. Figure 2 in the appendix is an example of such a form. These can be time savers, and if well designed they will supply all of the information that the graduate school needs without your having to write a letter or use the diverse forms that they may supply. You can also develop an application form to be filled out by the student requesting a reference as a convenient way of getting the information that you will need. As in the case of any important correspondence, always retain and file a copy of each letter of recommendation that you write.

If you are to work effectively with your students it is essential that you develop the proper rapport with them both collectively in class and individually.

An effective rapport with a student requires that he feels able to communicate with you freely about any matter. In order to develop this confidence, it is essential that you treat all student communications with you as private and confidential unless they clearly are not so intended. This means that without their express permission you do not repeat what they say to colleagues, administration, friends, or even your spouse.

While this proscription may seem obvious, sometimes when the seeker of information has some official or institutional status, the need for confidentiality may not be so apparent. Occasionally, for example, you may get a call from another college to which a student is seeking a transfer inquiring as to what his "real" mark was in a course in which his official grade was listed as a P. The proper answer to such an inquiry is a polite refusal to look beneath the recorded grade not only on the grounds of confidentiality but also because to do so would in effect nullify a pass/fail grading system.

Incidentally, when I advise students about taking courses on a pass/fail basis when they are eligible, I advise them against it. For one thing most people evaluating transcripts assume that all P's are really D's. Many of my students have elected P's at the beginning of a course that they feared would be difficult and then went on to do A work. You should ask the student who wants a P in every course that he doesn't think he can get an A in, what satisfaction there is in a "straight A average" if it has to be obtained in that manner.

You will also frequently have the occasion to tell students that it is a waste of time and money to drop a course, except for the most compelling reasons. I advise the student that he ought to fight it out and finish every course he starts. Course droppers are being trained to run away every time they are faced with some problem in life. This is extremely maladaptive training. What the student should be learning is how to seek out ways of solving his problems. The advisor has to remember that students, like professors, have mood swings and periodically get disgusted with their life situation and courses. These moods are transitory and will pass away. What the student really needs in these situations is a little encouragement and emotional support to get him over these rough spots. It would be nice if faculty had advisors to do the same for them during their low periods.

In all of your out of class relationships with students there are certain specific objectives to keep in mind. The first of these is to give your advisees only complete and accurate information. This will often involve your looking things up and carefully considering advice before you give it.

The second objective is to do nothing to destroy an effective working rapport with a student. The most effective working relationship with a student is based on mutual respect and confidence. However inane or unreasonable you may find some of your students' problems or demands, you have to learn to accept your students as they are and to work with them. Expressing anger or annoyance at a student is always counterproductive. It will not solve a problem but it will destroy rapport and make problem solving even more difficult. Students ought to be treated with the same amount of courtesy and consideration that we habitually display toward authority figures. This is not to imply that students ought to be permitted to abuse or otherwise take advantage of the faculty. It merely means that a line of acceptable behavior can be established and maintained while treating students in the same way that we would want to be treated in their place.

While relationships between students and faculty should be based on mutual courtesy, respect, and free communication, it is essential that these relationships be professional and not personal ones. There are many good reasons for avoiding personal relationships with students. For one thing, as a professor you will be called upon to evaluate the quality of a student's work and assign him a grade. It is difficult to be objective about personal friends and your class has a right to expect these decisions to be objective.

A second factor is the old adage that familiarity breeds contempt. There is a certain element of truth in this and supervising the work of someone that you are too friendly with can present many problems. It can be bad for student morale if they have the feeling that some people in the class have a special relationship with the instructor.

One type of situation that most instructors will experience at one time or another in their careers, will rapidly convince the beginning teacher to err on the side of being too formal in his relationship with students. This is the situation in which a student of the opposite sex develops a crush on you. This may involve what psychologists call transference, i.e., the student is transferring emotions from some more significant person in her life to the instructor. It may also result from the misinterpretation of a sincere professional concern for the welfare of the student and the instructor must be on his guard against this. Whatever it results from, this can be an extremely embarrassing and disruptive type of reaction. You will save yourself many uncomfortable moments if you learn to recognize these reactions early and are careful to do nothing to encourage them.

The question may be asked, if the student and instructor are age contemporaries what would be wrong with the development of a personal relationship between them? The answer is quite simple. It will destroy the professional relationship which must be of prime concern.

If the instructor wants to avoid undue familiarity with his students but at the same time wishes to maintain a pleasant working rapport with them, how does he manage to walk this tightrope? You will discover that students, like most people, constantly engage in limit testing. You simply have to learn to reinforce their acceptable behavior and fail to reinforce their unacceptable behavior. Assume, for example, that in a small seminar class you have a student about your own age who starts to call you by your first name. Having decided that this familiarity is beyond what you consider a good working relationship, you need not make an embarrassing issue over it. You simply keep referring to the student as Mr. Doe. In most cases he will take the hint. If he doesn't you can arrange a private conference and explain to him tactfully why you would prefer him to be more formal in class.

There are some ethical implications in the relationship between students and faculty. The most common ones involve research or work performed by graduate students.

The practice of some professors of taking a senior authorship on a published paper originally written by a student for a course is unethical, unprofessional, and generally deplorable. No professor ought to be listed as an author on a student's paper unless he has materially contributed to the article. If he did so contribute, the position of senior or junior author is based on the relative contributions made to the paper, not on the student-professor relationship.

If a professor has a research grant, a student assistant ought not to be expected to work on it unless he is paid at a rate commensurate with the value of his services. The fact that this work may have some educational value for the student does not justify a violation of the Thirteenth Amendment to the Constitution. What this common situation really involves is a conflict of interest between professor and student. As long as you are employed as a professor your relationship with your students is for the benefit of the student. Therefore it is improper to assign students any type of work that results in a financial or other benefit to yourself at their expense. It is a good rule not to do business with friends or relatives, and if you are a professor it would be wise to add students to the list.

A final area of student interaction that most professors will find themselves involved with at one time or another is the selection process or the interviewing of potential students.

At the present time, we are in the disgraceful position of rejecting 50 percent of the qualified applicants to our medical schools. Law schools and many graduate programs have equally depressing statistics. One program in clinical psychology that I am familiar with has had over 3,000 applicants for eight class places. With selection ratios like these, however dismal the prospects for deserving aspirants to these professions or for the public in dire need of their services, at least we should be assured of getting the best people in these professions, right? Wrong. Did the last young doctor, lawyer, or clinical psychologist that you consulted really strike you as the kind of person that you could entrust your medical, legal, or personal problems to with complete confidence? Why in the face of such high selection ratios don't we get a better quality of person in these important professions? Basically it is because we do not know how to select students.

How many people selecting applicants for a program in clinical psychology, for example, have ever sat down and listed what the personal qualifications of a good psychologist are? If they did, they might conclude that he ought to have at least most of the following characteristics: a good knowledge of psychology, reasonable intelligence, a liking for people and empathy with them, maturity, integrity, and motivation toward helping people.

There are, of course, many other personal characteristics that a good psychologist ought to have. However, none of these except for the first is highly correlated with scores on a graduate record exam. Schools that select students primarily on the basis of grades and graduate record scores are probably rejecting many potentially excellent professional students while accepting some of the worst of the lot.

The justification given by people who are unwilling to devote the time to do better evaluations is that it's expensive to have people flunk out of graduate school and that by selecting people with high scores and grades this pitfall can be avoided. It would seem to be a better idea to look for more than just grade point averages in the selection of students; if this means that the dropout rate will go up, this can be compensated for by accepting a larger entering class than would be expected to graduate. This would enable graduate programs to remain as financially effective as they presently are and at the same time remove the financial motivation for universities to graduate students who ought not to be admitted to professions involving human life and welfare.

An even better solution, of course, might be for the states to divert some of the money that they are currently investing in competing with private colleges into the creation of needed medical and graduate schools. This would probably be as effective in getting votes for politicians as building unneeded undergraduate facilities. However, it would have the dual advantages of providing needed professional training to worthy students now unable to attain it while at the same time it would not drive all of the private colleges into bankruptcy and ultimately force the creation of more state schools to service students formerly handled by these private colleges.

5.
Major Teaching Methodologies– The Tools of the Trade

Before I discuss the details of using specific teaching devices, I would like to consider the major types of techniques available to the instructor and to consider their relative advantages and disadvantages. These techniques are like a set of plumbers' tools, and a skillful teacher must know not only how to use them all but under what circumstances each is the method of choice.

Lectures are probably the most common undergraduate teaching device used and they have many advantages. First, they permit an instructor to precisely determine the content, the organization, the pace, and the direction of the course. Second, they are time efficient and will enable the maximum amount of material to be presented in a given number of class meetings. Third, they are ideally suited for a class of beginners, for the instructor, who presumably is an expert, controls the learning situation and the course content. Lecturing is probably the easiest method of teaching from the instructor's point of view as he has maximal control over the class proceedings. It is a good method to get your feet wet with.

Discussion classes and seminars are much more difficult to conduct. Here the problem is to get the group members to contribute while at the same time you keep the discussion confined to relevant material. The reason that this technique is so difficult is that the kind of passive behavior that the instructor must use to get a discussion going tends to open the gate for digressions from the topic, and the more active behavior necessary to control digressions may have the effect of stifling further discussion if not skillfully used.

Discussions and seminars are devices which permit students to learn not just from the instructor, as in a lecture, but more importantly from each other. It therefore follows that to be useful, a seminar must be composed of students having something to contribute to the group. Hence, this technique is of most value in advanced or graduate classes where each student may know some things that the others don't. Students, of course, may contribute to a seminar not only in the presentation of new facts but even more importantly in the presentation of different viewpoints and orientations. A seminar is the type of class where the instructor is likely to learn the most from his students.

Because the students are more active in a seminar than in a lecture, the seminar tends to be a good learning vehicle in spite of the fact that it is not as time efficient as a lecture and won't be able to cover nearly as much material. What it does cover, it will cover better.

Since the students are more active in a seminar it is obvious that they must be better prepared and that unless they have done the required readings the seminar will either fall flat on its face or turn into a quasi-lecture on the part of the one or two students who are prepared. Thus, not only must the instructor give assignments that will effectively prepare the students to contribute, but he must get the students to do them on time.

It may not be so obvious to the beginner, but in spite of his more passive role, the instructor must prepare just as adequately for a discussion class as for a lecture. Actually he must be better prepared, for he, too, is often called upon to contribute, and he will have to jump in to fill gaps or correct errors in topics that the students, not he, have brought up.

Students will enjoy a well-run, provocative discussion class as it is relaxed and informal and they have the opportunity for maximum participation and control. A not so well-run discussion can be boring and tedious and a real drag to all concerned. Like any class it's important to get it started off on the right foot because once it starts to go sour it will be difficult to correct things.

There will be occasions when it will be desirable to combine the techniques of the lecture and the discussion in the same course. In some schools large classes in introductory courses are broken down into a number of small recitation groups meeting one or more times a week to permit students more access to an instructor for questioning and interaction. Often the instructor of these discussion groups will be a graduate assistant or some person other than the principal lecturer.

This is an attempt to gain the advantages of a lecture without its drawbacks in the form of reduced opportunity for questioning and student-instructor interaction. This technique will be most effective if the lecturer and the discussion leaders coordinate well with each other so that the discussions are in track with the lectures and supplement them. It is also important that the lecturer get sufficient feedback from the discussion leaders so that he can modify his lectures if necessary to be more responsive to the classes' needs. For example, the lecturer may discover that certain material was unclear to most of the class and requires further elaboration or explanation.

The most difficult type of combination arises when the same instructor finds it necessary to both lecture and conduct discussions in the same course. For example, in a course in experimental psychology in which the students are expected to do research you may want to spend the first quarter of the term lecturing on the elements of good experimental design and the next quarter on a discussion of what types of experiments the class might be interested in doing. What makes this combination of techniques difficult is that during your lectures you have conditioned the class to become passive and to sit back and watch you work. Now suddenly you must shift the burden of performance from you to them, and this prior conditioning will work against you.

This problem will be minimized if you are a good enough lecturer to prevent the group from becoming unduly passive during your lectures. Another approach is to divide up the class meeting time from the beginning of the term into a lecture and a discussion period to prevent this expectation set from developing.

A third common teaching method in addition to lectures and discussions is the use of laboratory work. This is a potentially useful device but it is probably the most misused technique of all. I have taken innumerable laboratory courses, both in engineering school and in psychology, most of which were a total waste of time. The reason for this was in most cases the lack of consideration on the part of the instructors of the specific goals of laboratory work.

The real value of a laboratory course to a nonprofessional student of a subject is to make the lecture material clear by providing concrete and practical applications of abstract principles. If this is the goal then the lab must be coordinated with the main course, and not be completely independent of it. It may be desirable at times to have laboratory work precede a lecture in order to lay a foundation for it. In the rare cases where this is so, this time sequence should be the result of a deliberate decision on the part of the instructor and not the result of happenstance or poor course design or coordination, which is usually the situation when a laboratory and a lecture section are out of phase.

Laboratory work ought to be selected for its illustrative value and should be no more time consuming than necessary. Cookbook chemistry labs, for example, where the student is given no reason for what he is doing in each step of the procedure and where there is no tie-in with his lecture work, fail to attain the goal of supplementing the lectures. Such laboratory courses probably turn off many potential chemists early in their careers.

If a laboratory course is part of a sequence of professional studies such as an engineering or a postgraduate psychology program, then the lab has another legitimate function: to train the student in the techniques of his trade and to give him some practical experience. Thus, it makes a great deal of sense to require a doctoral student in psychology to learn to write an experimental report in accordance with the standards required by psychological journals. Whether this makes sense for an undergraduate psychology major who wants to be a lawyer is another question, although in my view it may be justifiable since the requirement is not unduly onerous and people should not be encouraged to close out their career choice options while still undergraduates.

While not a specific teaching technique, the inductive method of teaching is worthy of some consideration. Inductive teaching is basically the case study method used in most law schools. Here the student or the instructor recites cases from which general principles are ultimately derived. This method is also used by some psychology teachers who recite on a series of experiments performed and their results. Inductive teaching is probably the most time inefficient method of teaching ever devised by the mind of man. Its proponents argue for it on three basic grounds:

In the first place they point out that the material presented actually defines the subject matter of the course, i.e., the experimental work in learning *is* the psychology of learning, and the law cases deciding constitutional issues *are* constitutional law. In the second place inductive teaching gives a professional student a chance to develop needed professional skills, i.e., a lawyer must learn how to read a law case and cull the operative principles of law in it from the dictum. A third useful function of the inductive method is that it forces a student to think and, hence, is a more active type of learning experience than having principles spoonfed to him in a straight lecture.

My personal view, after having been exposed to a great deal of inductive teaching as a student, is that the role of case material or experimental evidence in a course is rendered more effective when it is used by an instructor to illustrate principles that he has presented or to raise questions about such principles, rather than to develop those principles *ab initio*.

As to the argument that certain professional students, such as law students, require training in the reading of cases and in the gleaning of principles from this material, this is unquestionably true to a certain extent. However, if a law student really required three years of training to learn "how to read a case," I would be inclined to question his intellectual fitness to become a lawyer.

Incidentally, combinations of the foregoing techniques can provide a needed change of pace for a class and even the inductive method can prove useful when used on occasion in the context of a lecture class.

It is not important that the reader agree with my opinions or prejudices regarding any of the foregoing matters, but he should be aware of the advantages and limitations of all of these techniques and know when each of these techniques may be used with maximum advantage. While each of us will be more comfortable with one or more of the above methods than the others, a good teacher is able to use all of them effectively. Ideally the choice of technique should be based on the usefulness of the method for a particular application rather than on the instructor's own personal limitations. While it may not be realistic for the beginner to expect such versatility of himself until he has acquired a considerable amount of experience, if he is afraid to try anything new for fear of failure this experience will never be acquired.

If a particular technique seems appropriate to your class,

don't hesitate to give it a try. If you prepare a course conscientiously, you will discover that things usually work out much better than you had anticipated. An occasional failure is a necessary ingredient for professional growth and should not deter you from trying new methods. There is only one way to go through life without ever experiencing a setback or a failure, and that is to do nothing.

6.
Preparing and Delivering Good Lectures

The ability to prepare and deliver a quality lecture is a core skill that most of an instructor's other teaching techniques are based on and hence it deserves special attention.

A lecturer can be looked upon as a device that an engineer would call a "black box." He receives many inputs and generates certain outputs from them. The inputs consist of a large variety of facts and theories which have a tendency to be dull, complicated, and unrelated. The output consists of a selection of the most pertinent of these facts and theories which have been transformed in such a manner as to maintain their accuracy but to render them interesting, clear, related and integrated. This in a nutshell describes the general goals of a good lecturer.

There are three steps involved in the preparation and delivery of a good lecture:

1. becoming an expert in the subject matter of the lecture
2. preparing the lecture
3. delivering the lecture.

The first step was discussed in Chapter 3 and the remaining two steps will be dealt with in the present chapter.

45

Preparing a Lecture

As a result of your research you will have available a set of notes and materials covering the subjects to be discussed in the lecture. If the articles you have reviewed are lengthy or contain detailed facts or data, it will prove useful to photocopy the pertinent sections. This will permit you to do the actual work of preparing the lecture in the comfort of your own office without having to run back to the library constantly to look up something you neglected to jot down. Even if you do not use the bulk of the details copied, it is handy to have this back-up material should students ask detailed questions about your talk.

Before you prepare a lecture, mull over the material you've collected. Ideas need time to germinate, so allow yourself enough time to permit adequate consideration and thought between data collection and the deadline by which you must prepare a lecture.

With experience you will be able to estimate how much information can be presented in a given lecture period, and you will learn to select which material to use and which to leave out. Beginners tend to include too much material in a lecture, and when they discover that they can't possibly cover everything, they become panicky. Don't be upset if you find yourself having to omit material during a lecture; your class will never be aware of the problem. A more serious difficulty will arise if you haven't included enough material. The way to prevent running out of things to say is to always have enough back-up material available in case your lecture goes faster than you had anticipated. Even if you never use this material, having it available will give you confidence and having considered additional material will make what you do present even better.

After deciding on the major points that you are going to present, make a rough outline of the most effective order of presentation. Some people like to make this major outline on index cards, for convenience in changing the order of the points, but I have found it more convenient to simply make a few successive outlines, as at this point in your preparation there isn't much on paper anyway. The choice is simply a matter of personal taste. For each major area in your outline, mull over how you can introduce it and how it can be tied in with what came before. Then continue to outline the secondary points under each of these major topic areas.

Next, prepare a final outline of all the major, secondary, and tertiary points to be covered in your talk. This is a road map; it shows you where you are going and how you are going to get there. I have found that this outline should be triple spaced as you will use it to fill in the details of your talk.

If possible sit on the final outline for a week or two while you are mulling it over and collecting specific examples and illustrations for each of the points made in it. You will also need introductory and concluding remarks, although if the lecture is to occur within the context of a course these may be minimal. Nevertheless, it is helpful to state what you are going to cover at the beginning of a lecture or whenever a new topic is introduced, just as it is useful to give a course outline at the beginning of a term. This type of preview prepares the class for where you are going and makes it easier for them to follow you.

Once these details are inserted in the final outline, you have in fact prepared a basic lecture. Before finalizing it, you may wish to spend as much time as you have available in thinking about it and improving on it by the reordering of sections or the including or excluding of additional material. If your subject permits, a lecture ought to be organized into blocks with pick-up points so that if students have lost you without saying so they have an opportunity to catch up.

Having the basic lecture prepared, you are now in a position to see if it will be more effective if you use visual aids, handouts, or other materials. Unless these materials have a specific purpose don't use them as they can compete with you for the student's attention.

Work out in your lecture notes any complicated diagrams that you may have to put on the blackboard. A good lecture is not the place for free association in any of its elements. While the quality of a lecture is directly related to the amount of care taken in its preparation, a good lecture must seem spontaneous and extemporaneous. For this reason it is better not to write lecture notes in speech form. The beginner may want to do this because it gives him confidence, but the danger is too great that his nervousness in appearing for the first time before a class may cause him to read to the students. This could prove a total disaster.

As a compromise you might write out a speech and rehearse it with your spouse, friends, or on a tape recorder, but if you're going to bring the text with you to class keep it in your briefcase and work from a detailed outline.

The purpose of your lecture notes or outline is:

1. to guide you in your lecture and to keep you on course
2. to provide you with detailed facts as needed
3. to give you confidence.

To serve these ends an outline is best spaced so that it can be referred to rapidly at a glance. It may be helpful to mark it up with multicolored pencils to supplement the subordination and organization of ideas provided by indentations and underscorings.

A good lecturer constantly revises his lecture notes right up to the time that he gives the lecture. Over the years your notes will become so marked up with notations that they must be retyped periodically to keep them readable. When you teach a course often enough, you will begin to find yourself using your notes more to review before a class than for reference during the class itself. It is important to remember that even the best prepared lecture must be constantly revised as relevant material becomes available or as the generation gap inevitably whittles away at what once were appropriate illustrations and anecdotes.

If your notes are detailed, and they should be, numerous marginal topic titles are useful in helping you find things in a hurry. No matter how often you teach a course it is a good practice to read over your notes just prior to a class, but never do more than glance at them occasionally during a lecture.

DELIVERING A LECTURE

Preparing a lecture is the work part of the job, delivering it is the fun part. If you've done a good job of preparation, you can have confidence that the lecture will go well. If you haven't, you will soon discover that the best teacher in the world is no better than his material.

The first thing you must do in the initial meeting with a class is to establish a rapport with the students. What kind of a rapport you will want is a function of your own personality and your style of teaching, but establishing this rapport is the most important thing that you will ever do with a class. If you get the proper type of rapport going for you, you can do anything with the group and if you don't get it you can do nothing. By a rapport is meant a working relationship wherein you and the class clearly know what to expect of each other and what your respective rights and obligations are.

Classes have personalities collectively over and above that of individual members. Some classes are responsive and accepting, others are more critical. Some have a better sense of humor than others. Whatever your particular class's personality, you have to learn about it and how to live with it from the onset just as the class must learn to understand and accept your personality.

If you do not set out deliberately to establish the ground rules under which your course is to be conducted and if you fail to tell the students what they may expect of you and what you in turn will expect of them, it doesn't mean that you will not establish some kind of rapport with the group anyway. What it means is that the relationship that will be established between you and your class is based on accidental circumstances instead of your deliberate planning and will probably not be the kind that you need to function with maximum effectiveness.

In my opinion the atmosphere most conducive to learning is a relaxed one. This cannot be attained if you fail to inform your students at the onset quite candidly what you will and will not accept with regard to their work and behavior.

You will soon discover that no matter how good or how bad a job you do in any course, there will always be some students who think you are great and some who think you are terrible. Not satisfying all your students may hurt a little, but you would do well to remember that the reason that you can never do this is that students are individuals and each has a need for a different type of instructor. Better students can work effectively with a wider variety of teachers while poorer students may need a specific type of teacher in order to do well. The same is true of professors. An inexperienced professor may need a specific type of class personality in order to feel secure while a more experienced one can enjoy dealing with a wider variety of classes.

The most important thing to remember in delivering a lecture is that you must interact with your audience, not just talk at them. This is why it is so ineffective to read lecture notes. Interacting with a class means not only answering questions when they arise but observing your students and getting feedback as to how they are following the lecture. Without having to be told by student questions, a good lecturer knows if a class is following him intently or is bored and confused. He not only notices this but responds to it by slowing down, backtracking, or elaborating when necessary. He keeps his class actively involved in the lecture by rhetorical or actual questions and by his response to student reactions. He makes even a lecture an active participatory experience for all members of the class. A really great speaker like the late President Franklin Roosevelt can give every member of the largest audience the feeling that he is speaking personally to him.

Incidentally, you probably remember from your student days just how bad student talks can be, even those of good students with outgoing personalities. The reason for this is both simple and instructive. These speakers were primarily concerned with impressing the instructor with how well-prepared they were and how much they knew about their subject. Hence, they ignored the audience and directed their remarks only to the professor. This is a cardinal sin. Always remember that your class is the sole reason for giving your lecture and you will be off on the right foot.

Interacting with a class in its fullest sense means considering the needs of every member in the class. This can tax the skill of the best of lecturers. Even graduate classes are highly heterogeneous in their makeup with respect to abilities and interests. Thus, a good lecture must be a compromise between the requirements of the best student, who may be bored with too rudimentary an explanation or too slow a pace, and the poorest, who may be overwhelmed by anything more. The instructor must give something to each and at the same time consider the requirements of the other. This is why teaching never gets boring; it presents a challenge to attain a standard that the best of us can only hope to approximate in practice.

Until you develop some experience in lecturing, you will discover that the timing of your lectures is never what you expected it to be when you prepared them. Usually the beginner finds that his lectures go too fast. This may be a sign of nervousness. Appearing alone in front of a large class looking expectantly at you provides a powerful motive for you to do something, and it is embarrassing to be silent for even an instant under such unfamiliar circumstances.

Talking too fast can also be a sign of following your notes too closely. If you are lecturing so fast that the students can't possibly take notes from you, they will naturally assume that you don't intend the material to be taken down so they will stop taking notes. When this happens, of course, there is even less of a restraining influence on you so you go zooming through the lecture.

Sometimes lecturing too fast may result from your fear of forgetting a particularly cogent point that just occurred to you if you don't get it right out. It is a golden rule never to go faster than your particular group can follow. Your best lecture will be lost forever on your class if they don't get a chance to jot notes down. When you find your lecture moving too fast, there are some things that you can do to slow it down and to give the class a chance to catch up. You can, for example, write major points on the blackboard or make more detailed diagrams if appropriate. You can ask questions of the class relevant to the material. You can also bring in some of your back-up material and stories. What you should not do is to talk about trivia or wander from the topic under consideration.

If, on the other hand, you find that your lecture is going too slowly this is an excellent sign. It usually means that you are interacting with your class. You did not do this when you timed your lecture by reciting it at your spouse. Don't worry if it looks as though you are not going to be able to get through all of your material. It is not important that you do. What is important is that what you cover is covered well.

The nervous beginning lecturer can pick out a sympathetic looking student to talk to for the first few minutes until he begins to feel at home with the group. Every class, no matter how hostile looking, always has at least one such person, but don't neglect the rest of the class and talk only to him for the rest of the lecture. Just come back to him occasionally when you feel the need for moral support.

With a little experience you will soon discover that no matter how badly your lecture goes nobody ever gets up and leaves, makes nasty remarks, or throws things at you. Your class has had years of experience in classroom deportment and courtesy and it's all working for you. In over ten years of teaching literally thousands of students and during the height of the period of student protest during the 1960s I never experienced a single case of a disruptive student and neither will you unless you invite such conduct by manifesting a lack of respect either for yourself or your students.

Even though you have prepared a well-planned lecture, your goal of involving and informing your students can only be attained by capturing the attention of your class. Attention requires effort to maintain even on the part of experienced students. The more you maintain class interest, the less effort the students need to be attentive.

The most fundamental principle in giving an interesting lecture is that it must be fun for you. If you enjoy it, your class will; if you don't, they won't. This is the essence of good teaching. Lecturing is an exercise in mutual reinforcement between you and your class. Interest is a contagious thing and so is its absence. It's hard to give a good lecture about something that you are not interested in. It is more than hard; it is impossible.

No one can be interested in something that he doesn't understand. This is why the organization of your lecture is so important. This organization and the concrete examples that you use to illustrate otherwise abstract principles serve not only to clarify the material, but also to help maintain student interest.

If for some reason you wanted to destroy student interest as rapidly as possible there are several tested and proven techniques that can be used. These are even more effective if used in combination with each other:

1. Read or recite your lecture to assure that it is totally unresponsive to your class.
2. Talk at instead of to students. Better still, talk down

to them. Try such expressions as "if you were a group of professional students, of course, I'd go into this in greater depth."

3. Wander or drift from your outline so that neither you nor your students know where you are or where you are going.

4. Overload the class members with so much material in a short period of time that they will have to lose you. Follow this up by avoiding pick-up points in your lecture so that they never have a chance to get back on board.

5. Be afraid to commit yourself and your personality to the class and speak in a monotone, carefully avoiding saying or doing anything controversial.

6. Be bored yourself. This is the most effective technique of all.

One of the best ways of learning to become a teacher is to study other teachers and notice what you like or dislike about what they do. Thinking back on your own professors, you will discover that you can learn just as much about teaching from the poor teachers as from the good ones. It is not enough just to notice what they did that was or wasn't effective; it is also necessary to consider your own personality and to decide which of these techniques that were effective for others would also be effective for you.

There are some things that others may be able to do effectively that you can't do and vice versa. The way to find out what you can do successfully, of course, is to try techniques used by others that appear to be worthwhile and evaluate the results that you obtain from them. However, you must always keep in mind that whatever you do, if it is to be successful, must fit in with your own personality. Nobody can be happy wearing a persona continuously, and if you are to enjoy teaching, what you do must feel right and comfortable for you. You have a unique personality; learn to get the most mileage out of it. You can often turn what may appear to be a handicap, such as poor diction, into a unique teaching asset if you will learn to capitalize on it. Anything out of the ordinary student expectations in a classroom situation has a certain potential for generating interest if handled with restraint and good taste.

There are certain specific techniques that can be quite useful to a lecturer. The question is the first and most versatile of these. You may ask questions seeking a response or you may use rhetorical ones that you answer yourself, but in both cases they serve the function of motivating the students to think about the material. If not directed at a specific individual they put no one on the spot and cause no embarrassment. The use of a question directed at an individual for the purposes of embarrassing him as a reprimand for some behavior that the instructor disapproves of is to be avoided. It is an abuse of the instructor's position as leader of the class and will quickly destroy rapport with the group as most students will recognize the basic unfairness of this type of behavior on the part of the instructor.

Avoid negatively reinforcing students who give answers other than the one that you are looking for in response to your questions. This is an ideal way to train a class never to volunteer an answer to any future questions you may ask.

On difficult or key points during your lecture always pause and ask if there are any questions to be sure the class is with you. On other occasions you will ask questions of your class to get information. For example, if there is a point that you have never understood about the subject you might try candidly mentioning this to your class and asking if any of them can supply an answer. You will be surprised how often you will get a good answer, and even if you don't, such a question is good for your rapport with the class for it demonstrates your respect for student opinions. The most productive student-teacher relationship is based on mutual respect.

Questions are also useful ways to make statements less abruptly and to make these statements easier for the other person to accept without seeming to back down from his previous position. If he chooses not to accept a statement couched in the form of a question, you at least have avoided a direct confrontation with him on the issue. Such confrontation may not be desirable, particularly in a classroom situation.

Humor is another effective classroom device. It can be used to break up a difficult sequence of material, to prevent or overcome boredom, or to bring back a class after you've lost it. Its most productive use is to make a point.

To be effective classroom humor must:

1. fit in with your ability and personality. (Some people shouldn't be permitted to tell jokes.)
2. be relevant to what you are discussing.
3. be appropriate to the dignity of your position and the restrictions of good taste.
4. be funny.

With regard to the last requirement sometimes a story can be so bad that it's good. The danger in classroom humor is that if you are effective with it you will be so well reinforced by your class's response that you can easily lose sight of the fact that you are not a nightclub act and you may get carried away and overdo it.

To get class participation in a lecture in the form of questions or comments, try inviting this participation periodically and then pause long enough to give the students a chance to respond. When they do, it is essential that you always reward them for their effort by listening fully and attentively to them without interruption. Never fail to recognize a cogent point made by a student as such and never show impatience with a student question or response no matter how inane it may seem. Once the students learn that class participation is always positively accepted the more timid ones will overcome their initial reticence and assume a more active role in the class.

With respect to visual aids, such as charts, slides, and physical demonstration items, it is my opinion that in most cases they are used inappropriately. To the extent that they are effective in attracting interest they will compete with your lecture unless you carefully time their usage. Don't give out handouts until just before you intend to refer to them and keep demonstration materials out of sight until you are ready to use them.

Visual aids should only be used when there is a specific purpose for them, such as the presentation of tables of data that you will refer to or charts and diagrams of much greater complexity or accuracy than you could reasonably expect to sketch on the blackboard. Before using any apparatus or materials for the first time you should carefully rehearse so that your class is not distracted from what you are saying by your fumbling efforts to manipulate the equipment.

A really good lecture, like a work of art, should be subtle. The techniques that you may use should not be obvious as students, like most people, will resent it if they feel that they are being manipulated. Your organization and planning should be obvious in your student's notes but not in your manner of delivery. In the last analysis no one can tell you how to prepare and give a lecture any more than someone could tell an artist how to paint a great picture. A lecture is too personal a thing and it must be designed to fit your own personality, abilities, and limitations as well as the requirements of your subject and students. However, the foregoing guidelines will prove useful in getting started in the right direction.

7.
Leading Productive Discussions

The major problem in running a discussion is to get the individual members of the class to open up and contribute. You do this by making them feel comfortable in the class environment and by effectively reinforcing them when they do make contributions to the proceedings.

With respect to the requirement of making the students feel comfortable in the group situation, a great deal depends on establishing an informal and accepting atmosphere. No student should ever receive an adverse reaction from you for anything he says in a discussion, and at times you may have to take a hand to support him, morally at least, if class reaction to his statements becomes unduly adverse. Students who are well prepared for a class will usually·have a much lower anxiety level about contributing than those who are unprepared, so anything that you can do to assure adequate student preparation will help to get and to keep the discussion going. For example, in a proper situation you might let it be known that a certain number of examination items will be based on the readings.

Never tell a student that the statement that he has just made clearly demonstrates that he didn't do the assignment unless you are engaged in an experiment to see how rapidly you can stifle all class discussion. Also never show annoyance or boredom with any student contribution either by word or facial expression. The first thing that must be done to get a discussion going is to encourage individual group members to start talking. When they do this they must be reinforced for their responses so that they will continue to make them. Later when they become more comfortable with you and with each other it is possible to become more selective in your reinforcements.

How do you reinforce a student? There are a variety of ways such as a nod, a smile, or a statement that the point he raised was a good one (if it was), but they all boil down to some expression of interest or appreciation on your part. To be effective, reinforcement has to be sincere and appropriate to the contribution. Initially you may have to be on your toes to avoid missing any responses that should be reinforced appropriately. The most effective reinforcement is that which the instructor will give spontaneously in the course of interacting with the group as opposed to deliberately manipulative responses made by him.

Conducting a discussion class in the proper physical environment is half of the battle. If you have been assigned a standard lecture room for a seminar, the very first thing to do is to call the registrar's office and get the room changed. The ideal room for a seminar is one that is just large enough for the group and is provided with a conference table.

There are several things wrong with trying to hold a seminar in a lecture hall. For one thing, if you are standing in front of the class all of their past experience in classroom situations has conditioned them to sit back passively and wait for you to do something. When they do talk, you will notice that they don't talk to each other but to you and it will take a great deal of effort on your part to get them to talk to each other directly and not through you.

There was a time when I was retained by a local manufacturing plant to give a series of lectures on Industrial Psychology and Leadership to a group composed of supervisory personnel, as part of an in-house training program. The lectures were two hours in duration and were interrupted by a ten-minute coffee break at the midpoint. The talks were given in a special lecture room set up in the plant.

Two things became noticeable from the onset. In the first place, even though the lectures were adequately planned they tended to go much too fast. In the second place, even though the class seemed interested in the material the amount of class participation was minimal.

A little thought disclosed the reason for the lectures' going so rapidly. In addition to the physical facilities' being inappropriate to invite discussion, unlike a group of college students, the class was not going to be tested on the material and therefore they weren't concerned with taking extensive notes and did not mind the accelerated pace. The lack of student discussion and questions, of course, compounded the problem. In view of the small amount of class participation the reader may be wondering where I ever got the idea that my group was interested in the course. That they were was made obvious by the fact that I never got a chance to get a cup of coffee during the break as I was swamped with students asking questions or wanting to talk about the material.

One day the problem of low class participation was solved by simply calling the coffee break a little early and never reconvening the class. The group had a one-and-a-half-hour coffee break and discussion period.

Another problem in getting a discussion going that is made worse in a lecture hall is the habit that students have acquired in the first grade, of raising their hands to ask a question or to speak. It will take you a long time to extinguish this habit and you might effectively make a little joke out of it.

One of the big advantages of a conference table is that students who might be a little timid about speaking before a group don't have to stand up to talk. If you don't have a round table be sure not to sit at the head of the table or at any other prominent position such as the middle. This can be almost as stifling to the initial efforts of your students at speaking as your being in the front of a lecture hall.

One of the concerns of the beginning seminar leader is what to do if the group clams up and nobody says anything. This is likely to occur during the early sessions before the ground rules are firmly established and the class gets rolling. It may occur to a lesser extent at the beginning of each period. It is important to realize that there is a certain warm-up period required before any class gets moving and this is true both for lectures and discussions. This is why there is no such thing as a ten-minute break, for after this break it may take you another five or ten minutes to pick up momentum again. Thus, if the total period for a lecture or seminar does not exceed two hours it is better when possible to permit smoking or eating in class than to break it up in the middle. Of course, if the class isn't going well a ten-minute break might be useful in permitting you another chance to start off on the right foot.

This warm-up effect can be seen not just in the classrooms but in practically any type of task you undertake. It may take you almost as much time to get into the mood to prepare a lecture as the actual preparation does. Some people can't really get down to work in preparing for a course until shortly before the start of the term. The imminence of the class evidently supplies the necessary motivational factor.

It is because of this need for a class as well as the instructor to have a warm-up period at the start of a class session that the experienced professor will not tell any of his better stories or make any important points during the first few minutes of a class session but will wait until he builds up a little momentum.

It is interesting to notice that just before each period there will come a time when all of the student talking and shuffling of papers in even the largest of classes will suddenly stop and the class will look at you expectantly. This is the proper time to start the class. If you start before or after this point in time it will take longer to get going.

There are a number of effective ways of getting people to contribute to a seminar. The first and most basic method is to simply remain silent and give them a chance to say something. This can be more difficult than it sounds, particularly for an instructor who has a lot of ideas about the subject and who is used to the more active process of lecturing. However, a conscientious effort on the part of such an instructor not to intervene unless necessary will pay big dividends.

Sooner or later you will be confronted in one of your lecture classes with the chronic questioner who is constantly disrupting the class with irrelevant or poorly timed questions. Often he will cause a great deal of resentment on the part of his fellow students. In a seminar, however, this student may prove more of an asset than a liability, for here his fellow students are not helpless and his comments may evoke a great deal of discussion.

While an overtalkative student may help to stimulate discussion, the opposite is usually true for an overtalkative instructor. For one thing, being a professor cloaks you and your remarks with some aura of authority and many students will be reluctant to disagree with you publicly about matters in which you are supposed to be an expert. Also due to the prior training of students, an overly active instructor tends to make a class more passive.

A classic bit of advice given to a young trial lawyer is equally applicable to a discussion leader. Never lose an opportunity to keep your mouth shut. Some people have difficulty following this advice because as previously mentioned they find it embarrassing to appear before a group, looking expectantly at them, without saying or doing something. This is of course somewhat difficult because there is a powerful motive provided by the group situation, but herein lies the value of your silence in getting the group to talk. It is also uncomfortable for the class members and they too are motivated to act. The only difference is that you are aware of this more explicitly than they are and if you determine to outwait them you will invariably succeed in eliciting student comment.

Another way of getting a class to respond is to ask questions. Here you must be careful to do it in a way which will not single out or embarrass any individual. It is preferable at first to ask questions of the group rather than specific individuals. If it becomes necessary to question individuals always confine yourself to questions that you are certain they can answer without difficulty. Questions requiring specific information should never be asked of individuals. Your goal is getting the group to open up and you can't accomplish this by making people apprehensive. This will have exactly the opposite effect.

An effective way of getting student participation is to play the devil's advocate by making outrageous statements or questioning the basic assumptions of the group. For example, if the group is discussing Freud's idea of psychic determinism, which holds that thoughts are just as subject to the laws of cause and effect as are physical acts, you might question what sense it makes to put people in jail for committing crimes if they are helpless to control their thoughts and behavior, and you might advocate the abolition of the criminal law. On the other hand, if you are considering the relative deterrent value of the severity of punishment for a crime versus the certainty of punishment you might throw out Justice Holmes's statement to the group wherein he suggested the idea of hanging every fourth pickpocket and letting the other three go free.

Another useful technique that can also be used during lectures as well as discussions to start class participation is to ask the class to name things which you then list on the board. For example, in a human engineering course you might ask the class in how many ways machines are superior to people or vice versa.

This method has several advantages. For one thing, it starts the group participating in a fairly directive manner.

Secondly, the ideas expressed are theirs, not yours, and hence are more important to them than anything that you might spoonfeed them. Thirdly, you will find that quite often the class will come up with a few good points that you didn't think about. If the class omits anything that you consider important you can, of course, always add this material later.

While the need for the discussion leader to remain unobtrusive has been emphasized it must also be pointed out that he is still a member of the group and has an obligation to make significant contributions to the discussion when appropriate. He also has certain other more specific duties.

While the instructor's prime function is to get the discussion going and to keep it on course, he should contribute additional factual or theoretical material that is relevant to points raised by students if it becomes apparent that the students themselves won't.

During the course of the seminar the instructor must be accepting of whatever student opinions are expressed, although he may express professional disagreement with them. He cannot permit factual error to go without correction, however. This correction should be made tactfully, but it must be made.

The group leader must be prepared to fill in gaps in the discussion and to keep it going with prodding questions when necessary while at the same time taking care not to take over the class to the exclusion of students wishing to say something.

The matter of how far to permit digressions to continue is a question of good judgment. If a discussion is productive and relevant to the course even though it may have strayed considerably from what you had planned, it might be wise not to interfere. Only when the class gets sidetracked with irrelevant and sterile material or student debate gets overly heated is interference justified. To a large extent the students should control the direction of a seminar.

A heated discussion among class members is a sign of a successful seminar and should not be interfered with unless it ceases to be productive or becomes personal. A good instructor will recognize the trend that an argument is taking and stop it before the participants themselves realize it is about to become personal.

You will know that you've had a successful session when the class doesn't want to stop at the end of the period or class members continue the discussion in the corridors.

8.

Problems in Teaching

The major problems encountered in teaching can be divided into those with students and those with the course. Problems with students can be further classified as problems with students generally and problems with particular students. General student problems will be dealt with first.

Most problems with students occur within the context of a classroom situation. One of the most common problem areas is that of student questions. The first type of problem question is the one that is totally irrelevant to the material being discussed. Sometimes a question will be so confusing that you aren't sure whether it is relevant or not. In such a case always inquire further as to what it is that the student is actually asking. It is a waste of class time to answer the wrong question. If a question is clearly irrelevant the best way of dealing with it is to invite the student to discuss it with you after class. The same procedure should be followed if the student is so confused that he can't frame a question at all, unless you have reason to believe that enough of the class share this difficulty to make it worth while to go over the material again and then see if the student can either follow it or formulate a satisfactory question.

If you are asked a question that you don't know the answer to, as you unquestionably will be from time to time, the best course to follow is to admit that you don't know and undertake to find out by the next class meeting. If you have an opinion, you may make an educated guess provided that you label your response as such and undertake to check it out. As mentioned previously no professor can know the answer to every possible question, but if you find yourself being unable to answer too many it suggests that you have some brushing up on your material to do. If you have to respond this way often enough it will tend to discourage class questions as students will be anxious to avoid creating embarrassing situations. Probably the most frequent types of questions that you will be unable to answer will relate to either very specific or very recent studies. This again points up the need for a professor to be a lifelong student.

Often a student will ask a question about a point that you will cover later in the lecture or later in the course. In most cases it is a mistake to answer it prematurely as this will tend to cause you to digress from the point at hand and disrupt the organization of your lecture. The best approach is to tell the student that you will cover this point at some specific time and request him to renew his question at that time if you fail to answer it. Incidentally, remember this question and when you do cover the material asked about, refer back to the student's question and specifically answer it. This is a good public relations technique because it gives the student the feeling that he is known and considered important by you. Of course if the question raised involves not just the elaboration of some point, but requires an answer for the student to be able to understand the material presented, then it should not be deferred if it is possible to answer it. If an adequate answer requires familiarity with some material not yet covered, then some type of stopgap answer, subject to later elaboration, may have to be given at this time.

Occasionally a question will be asked concerning a point

which you are just about to make. This is an ideal question as it makes your lecture appear more responsive. Don't spoil this opportunity by saying that you were just about to discuss that subject but make your lecture material appear as a response to the question asked just as though you wouldn't have covered the material but for the question. The information you now give the student is more important to him because it has been given in response to his personal question. Your answer is now also a reinforcement for the students' response of participating in the class.

While disruptive college students are such a rarity in my experience as not to warrant considering them, there are certain other types of problem students. One of the most difficult to deal with is the persistent questioner. Often the frequency of this person's questions coupled with their irrelevance or speechlike qualities can be extremely disruptive to a lecture's organization and can cause a great deal of class resentment directed against the questioner. In dealing with such a student it is important to do nothing that will tend to inhibit other members of the class from asking questions, although often student reaction to the offender by itself may have this undesirable side effect. A golden rule is never to do anything to embarrass or negatively reinforce any question asker. It is also important to permit the excessive questioner enough freedom of operation before taking any kind of action, so that the other class members are likely to recognize the clearly excessive nature of his behavior and be unlikely to be deterred from asking legitimate questions themselves by any steps that you may take to remedy the situation.

As to what steps you can take without destroying your rapport either with the class as a whole or with the student in question, this is a function of your own personality and your relationship with the student concerned. A private and tactful talk with the offender may help, but great care must be exercised that the student is not given the impression that he is being rejected or reprimanded.

I had one case where a chronic questioner was literally infuriating the class with pointless and verbose questioning to the point that many of the students privately complained to me that I had to "do something" about it. However, no complainant when asked for suggestions had any specific ideas about what could be done. After wrestling with the problem for a while, I decided to pass out course rating forms to be filled in by the students in the middle of the term. Students were told that their views were being solicited on how well the course was going prior to the end of the term, when it would be too late to do anything about any problems.

In the course of reading some of the class comments back to the group, I included a half dozen or so comments concerning the excessive questioning which had been made by certain unnamed people (deleting the expletives of course). I also read their requests for the instructor to do something to stop this. These comments were then answered by defending the right of all students to ask questions and otherwise participate in the course. The questioner took the hint, a potentially destructive situation was avoided and the rest of the class was not inhibited from future participation.

It is important to bear in mind that if you are going to make an error in your interaction with a student always err on the side of underreacting. For example, if you are annoyed by the amount of questions asked by a student this is not really important. It is part of your job to cope with student questions. It is only when these questions reach the stage of annoying or hindering your other students that they become a problem that has to be dealt with. Often peer pressure alone will resolve this and similar problems without the need for any action on your part if you give it a chance to work.

How direct you can be with disruptive student private conversations in class is also a function of your rapport with the group. If you have a good enough one you can even say "shut up" in a nonoffensive, half joking manner, but here again it is the better policy to underreact. If you are dealing with a strange class at the beginning of the term you might try whispering for a few minutes to emphasize the need for quiet in a joking manner. When you attain my advanced age you can appeal as I occasionally do to the better nature of the offending students by imploring them to give you a break on the theory that you are a tired old man who can't talk any louder.*

The two major types of problem students that you will certainly encounter are the slow student and the unusually bright one. Even though there is less diversity in abilities among college students than you would expect to find in a high school or in a grammar school class most college and even graduate classes contain a heterogeneous group of students with respect to ability, interests, and motivation. Thus, as was mentioned earlier, the instructor is constantly faced with the dual problems of not losing the slower student while trying to arouse the interest of the brighter one and not boring the brighter student while trying to carry the less gifted one along with the class. This problem of student heterogeneity is one of the major advantages of small class sizes. It is not likely that colleges will ever introduce track systems such as those used in some elementary schools in an effort to reduce this problem of student variability, because no college is ever likely to admit that it accepts any but outstanding students. Class mix is one of the things that make teaching such an interesting challenge. A good teacher, while having to make compromises in material and pace, will attempt to bring almost everyone in the class through the course to some acceptable level of performance and at the same time give enough attention to the better students to make the course worth their while. A poor teacher will constantly aim at the class mean and will therefore lose both the poorer and the better students.

---

*Actually you don't have to be much older than thirty to use this technique. You will be appalled to discover how readily your class will accept this statement as literal truth!

Some ways of getting better students to extend themselves within a course are special projects or papers. Within a program, honors papers, assistantships, and tutoring opportunities are other vehicles to accomplish this purpose.

Poorer students may need a standing invitation to consult with you outside of class on the material. If the student is really in trouble with the course and requires more time than you can reasonably make available to him you may be able to arrange a symbiotic tutoring arrangement between him and a better student in the class. This will give the one the extra help he needs and the other an opportunity to learn through teaching, which is probably the most effective learning method known. This tutoring arrangement can and should be supplemented by periodic consultations with you on the part of either the student or his tutor.

Perhaps the most trying student to deal with is the grade collector. Often his neurotic preoccupation with getting A's is the result of the admissions policies of the graduate or professional schools to which he plans to seek admission. Sometimes it is also the result of having a perfectionist or compulsive personality. This person may effectively rob himself of an opportunity to acquire an education in college by carefully selecting a program of courses that he feels will facilitate his getting A's. If he can't avoid difficult courses, he will at least try to take them on a pass/fail basis. Often he will come to you with the attitude that he is entitled to an A in your course since he has never had any problem in any other course and if he's having one now it must be your fault. One often wonders how much of some "straight A" averages is based on ability as a student and how much is based on the ability to intimidate wishy-washy faculty members.

An occasional variation on this character is the student who must get an A in your course or he won't graduate, won't get into graduate school, or will be subject to some other grave traumatic effect. This student may couple his obsession over grades with a general inaptitude for either study or the course.

An example of this type is the student who has a 40 average in the course and comes to see you the day before the final asking if he can write a paper or do something to get an A.

These types of problems involving grading can be unpleasant because it is the ploy of the student to attempt to make you feel guilty concerning his grade, and unless you realize that a student grade is determined by the student and not by you, you may be unable to resist this type of unfair pressure.

Assuming that you have worked out a fair and equitable grading scheme (Chapter 9) and have applied it to your students with care and consideration and you have done a conscientious job in class during the term as evidenced by the performance of the rest of your class, then you ought to so advise the student and point out to him where the responsibility for his grades lies. It is not fair to the rest of your class to permit yourself to be bullied into giving a student a higher grade than his work warrants, simply because he is more aggressive than his classmates. This is not to say that you shouldn't try to help him to do better by pointing out more efficient study methods or areas in which he needs more work if he comes to you for timely consultation.

Students who become obsessed with grades may require help in changing their personal philosophies of life or their frame of reference and value systems that an instructor may provide. This type of student needs more adaptive ideas about what is and what isn't important in life. In extreme cases he may benefit from psychotherapy or counseling. It is important for the instructor to learn to distinguish between students who have a sincere neurotic preoccupation with grades and those who have learned that playing on the sympathies or guilt feelings of their professors is an effective way to raise their grade point average with a minimum of effort. The sincere group needs help and counseling. The manipulative group needs a firm No.

With respect to problems with the course there are several common ones that can be minimized with proper planning.

Teachers, like baseball players and people in general, have slumps where nothing seems to go right and it's hard to maintain interest in their courses.

Many of these down periods are simply due to the mood swings that all people experience, but occasionally there are more specific causes. One of the most common causes of poor course performance is the fact that you've taught the same course either for too long a time or at too frequent intervals. In general, the same course shouldn't be taught by a professor more than once a year unless some special situation within a department makes this necessary. This implies that a teacher must have prepared enough of a variety of different courses after a reasonable time on the job to permit this diversification. He must have enough courses prepared to fill out his program from year to year with sufficient variety to maintain his own interest and enthusiasm. If you are a bona fide specialist, and few people really are, you may be the only one in the department who can teach a particular course. If this happens to be a course which is constantly offered, term after term, you would do well to train a colleague in the area so that you are not always stuck with it.

The practice of some departments of treating some courses as though certain instructors had a property right in them is to be condemned. It is bad for the instructor teaching the course, who soon grows stale, and it is bad for the rest of the department, who are deprived of the opportunity to get into other areas and thereby grow professionally. If you are in a department that does not afford you a reasonable opportunity to diversify and teach new courses and which treats certain courses as though they belonged to particular faculty members you would do well to look for another job before your intellectual and professional growth is stifled to the point where you become incapable of doing anything new. This type of intellectual death can occur quite rapidly and many people fail to recognize it, thinking that lack of diversity and scope is a sign of expertise, which it most assuredly is not. Most of the real experts that I have met have always amazed me by the diversity and scope of their knowledge. It would be strange indeed if the kind of inquiring mind necessary to become an expert in any intellectual field could be confined to one small area of human knowledge.

As you add to your repertoire of course preparations you will soon discover that there are certain courses that you should not teach during the same semester. For example, it may be that your introductory course contains a lot of material covered in a more advanced course and you may experience great difficulty in remembering just what you covered in each class. If there is a direct overlap of some material, as is sometimes unavoidable, you may find yourself telling the same story to one group twice and omitting the material in the other group. This problem is particularly severe if you are unfortunate enough to teach two sections of the same course during the same term. This is a situation that you should avoid at all costs but occasionally it will happen to you, especially in introductory courses having large enrollments. There was one term when I had three sections of introductory psychology and the problem of remembering what was said to each class took on nightmarish proportions at times.

In this situation it is essential to keep the two classes in track with each other to the extent that holidays and snowstorms permit. This means that you must go slowly enough in the first class to be assured that the same material can be covered with the second group even if there are more questions or diversions in that class. If you are teaching two sections of the same course it will necessitate the preparation of two sets of examinations to assure that students who have friends in the first class have no advantage over their colleagues who do not. On the other hand a student who occasionally can't make a class on time may be able to attend the other session if you notify your students that there are two sections being given.

If I ever find a job in a college with an adequate budget

for educational devices one of the first things that I am going to do is to tape record every lecture in each of my courses. If you are just starting out in teaching and have only prepared a course or two it might be economically feasible for you to do this, and the idea has some attractive aspects to it. Primarily it will enable you to solve the problem of the student who was ill and missed a goodly portion of the course. About all you can do for him without a set of lecture tapes is to refer him to the notes of his fellow students or discuss with him whether or not he might be better off dropping the course. Not only can students who missed a substantial portion of the course be helped by being given a set of tapes to listen to but also students who missed just one lecture or who would like to hear certain material again can be accommodated.

Even if you can't afford to record an entire course, you should record your lectures periodically in any event, as it will give you an idea about the quality of your own lectures that you can get in no other way. Listening to a tape of your own lecture permits you to evaluate your performance against the same criteria that you used to rate your own professors when you were a student. If the practice of recording lectures ever becomes as widespread among instructors as it is among students, eventually some colleges may hit on it as a cheap way of interviewing or at least screening prospective faculty members, although it is to be hoped that they won't, as even a video tape of a lecture can't capture enough of the subtle interaction between a professor and his class to permit an adequate evaluation by a third party.

If you teach two sections of one course back to back you may often find yourself wishing that you could tape record the first session and just move your lips in time with the recording in the second session. Obviously you can't, but this points up the biggest problem in teaching two sections. The second group is entitled to as much interest, enthusiasm, and preparation on your part as the first group is. This means that even though you may plan to cover the same materials and illustrations you must still be just as spontaneous and responsive in the second class as you were in the first. This you will find takes a lot of skill, but the time you save in preparation as a result of just having given the same lecture can be used to work up the proper mental state for the job. The right attitude toward a class is similar to the right attitude to take when you are out with a member of the opposite sex; this present class is the only one you have and it's the most important one in the world.

While introductory classes by their nature tend to contain material that overlaps with many other courses that you may teach, it is a mistake to avoid them. Contrary to what many people seem to believe, it is not demeaning to an instructor to be given an introductory course to teach as opposed to a graduate or advanced course. Introductory courses actually require the best teachers, for it is here that the student's original attitude toward your subject is formed and where he often makes the decision to major in your field or not. Departments that routinely assign graduate students to teach introductory courses on the theory that the instructor doesn't have to know much are making a serious mistake, and unless the graduate student happens to be an excellent teacher (and some are) they are probably losing many potential majors.

Another serious problem that you are likely to encounter, particularly in a small department or if you are popular with your students, is the fact that the same students may take an undue number of courses with you. This is a problem both from the student's standpoint and your own.

From the point of view of the student he is being short-changed, for no matter how professionally competent you may be, the student is being deprived of the opportunity of being exposed to other viewpoints and opinions, which is the essence of what an education is about. The student will not learn anything that you don't know or believe to be important and this may cover a considerable amount of material even for the best of professors. If you are young and inexperienced, the situation is made even worse.

From the point of view of the instructor the problem of course material overlap is made more acute and he may be inhibited from telling his best stories since some of the students have heard them before. One excellent teacher once told me that he didn't mind repeating material in class because most of the students didn't learn it the first time anyway, but nevertheless this can be uncomfortable for a lecturer, and even the best joke is funny only once.

The reader may wonder why it is that overlap of material between courses can't be eliminated from an instructor's lecture notes. Often it can be and a good instructor will try to minimize it, but sometimes the same subject matter properly belongs in two different courses, especially if you realize that many students may not take both courses. Also there will be times when the instructor will have developed an effective way of introducing or illustrating a concept and he may be reluctant to use a second best approach in another course just for the sake of its being different.

If it is not practical to have a departmental policy limiting the number of courses that a student can take with the same instructor his advisor should at least point out these problems to him and seek to minimize the excessive exposure of a student to a particular instructor. Also advisors should specifically recommend that certain combinations of related courses be taken with different instructors whenever possible to minimize overlap of both material and orientation.

In some courses you may have just the opposite problem. If one course is truly a prerequisite for another, as for example, a course in statistics' being required for a course in experimental design, the best approach to take is to devote an initial lecture or two to a review of the prerequisite course to assure that class members who have taken the prerequisite with different instructors all start out with some common background.

This is, of course, only necessary if the prerequisite course is a true prerequisite and not merely a formal requirement as many so-called prerequisites really are.

While this chapter does not purport to deal with every possible problem that you will have with your students or your courses, you will find that it does cover the most common ones. The best sources of solution for the occasional unusual problem will be consultations with your colleagues and your own good judgment.

9.
Testing and Grading

One of the few unpleasant things about the educational system from the point of view of both the student and the instructor is the necessity to assign some grade to each student at the end of the term. I have often wondered if both students and universities might not be better off if this practice were abandoned altogether.

The practice of assigning grades is an academic tradition and primarily beneficial to graduate and professional schools in selecting future students. There is a substantial question as to whether or not the colleges have any real obligation to be an unpaid part of the selection organization of these other institutions, particularly in view of the great harm that grading systems can do to some students by misleading them into thinking that the proper goal of their college careers is to acquire a high grade point average rather than an education. Much psychological damage to students is caused by making unreasonable and unrealistic demands upon them to achieve high grades, and in the process most of the fun and excitement that should be a part of their educational experience is destroyed.

It may be argued that college degrees would be meaningless if they were to be issued on the basis of merely four years of class attendance without minimum grade requirements. This argument can be answered by inquiring, what does a college degree mean now? The purpose of a liberal arts college education is personal enrichment, not the attaining of vocational skills or recognition. How much or how little a student gets out of his education is basically his own business. The sooner that lazy or incompetent personnel managers understand that the presence or absence of a college degree has little to do with performance on most jobs, the sooner it will be possible to free academic institutions from the unwarranted and externally imposed requirement of being certifying agencies of vocational aptitude.

In a professional school program where students are being trained in specific vocational skills, as opposed to a liberal arts college, the case for grading to protect the public from incompetent practitioners becomes more compelling. Unfortunately both course grading and professional licensing examinations have not always proven adequate to this task.

While there may be serious problems created by examinations and grading, there are nevertheless some legitimate functions served by these procedures beyond helping graduate schools to make student selections or deferring to a long standing academic habit.

For one thing, examinations supply periodic motivation to students to review material and seek out solutions to unresolved problems. If an examination is well designed, it will also provide a certain amount of reinforcement to the students for their efforts in preparing for it. Conversely, poorly designed examinations—which permit an unprepared student to get an A or that cause well-qualified ones to do poorly—will rapidly train students not to study and will prove counterproductive. Another function served by a well-prepared examination is to provide a learning and integrating experience for the students. This is perhaps its most valuable use.

From the viewpoint of the instructor, an examination can be an extremely important source of feedback as to how well the course is attaining its objectives. It is probably a much more accurate index of instructor performance than any student comment is likely to be as it is uncontaminated by any halo effect, and over the years the instructor who maintains adequate records can notice trends of increased or decreased performance in a particular course.

It should be noted that all of the foregoing advantages of testing could be retained, if grading were eliminated, by simply using test scores as informal advisory information for the student's own use.

Since grading is not likely to be abandoned in the foreseeable future, in spite of experiments with such compromise devices as pass/fail grading, the instructor is going to have to learn how to live with this system, disruptive as it may be to optimal student-faculty relationships. The best policy to follow with respect to grading is to do a careful evaluation job within the context of a fairly designed grading system and then, having made a sound decision, do not change it unless a mistake is discovered in the factual basis of the decision, such as an error made in computing an average.

If you don't stand by your grading decisions when they are challenged, you will find yourself with an increasing number of such appeals each term. Even worse, you will be penalizing those less aggressive students who have accepted your decision concerning their grade.

Grades should be based on some specific criteria and the students ought to be informed of your grading standards at the beginning of the course. The more objective these standards can be made the better, because objective standards give students the feeling that they are being dealt with fairly. They also make grades easier to justify when they are questioned.

Before I discuss possible grading schemes, it is necessary to consider some of the examination devices that grades must ultimately be based on. Each of these devices, like the teaching techniques described earlier, has its own unique advantages and limitations.

The first device to consider is the essay examination. This type of exam can be used to give a student a chance to demonstrate his knowledge of the course material in some depth as well as his ability to integrate and organize the material. It is an easy type of exam to prepare from a production standpoint but care must be exercised to assure that the questions are specific enough to make it clear to the student who knows the material what specific aspects of the course he is to discuss.

Sometimes it is useful to limit the student's responses to relevant areas by asking him to contrast or compare differences and similarities between two or more specific concepts. Often a lot of needless writing may be saved if the student is requested to list relevant concepts, attributes, and so on. If the question is extremely specific, the student can be asked to limit his answer to one or two sentences.

The drawbacks of essay type questions are many. For one thing, they tend to be physically exhausting to the student. This effect is even more pronounced in the better prepared student, who often writes much too much in an effort to get all of his relevant knowledge onto his paper. Because of the time required to answer an essay question such an exam can cover only so much of the course content.

The most serious drawback of an essay question is that it must be marked subjectively. This means that your evaluation of the paper may be influenced by the student's writing and organizing ability or even his neatness under stress. While these are important, they may not be related to his grasp of the course material. This is what the examination is purporting to measure, and hence the validity of the examination tends to be lowered. Also a subjective mark is difficult to justify to a dissatisfied student, who is more likely to go away from a postexamination conference with you feeling less satisfied than if you were able to give him more specific reasons for his grade.

Because of the difficulty of grading essay examinations, you may find yourself tempted to try to set up objective standards for grading them. I know of no satisfactory method of making a subjective grading task objective. For example, there was a time when I used to write an answer myself for each question asked and then note the number of points made in this model answer. The student then received credit for each of these points made in his paper. This scheme ultimately had to be abandoned because it worked out that students who wrote concise, well-organized answers often missed several points and got poorer marks than students who wrote incoherent, redundant, rambling papers which accidentally stumbled on many of these points.

While essay questions must ultimately be marked on a subjective basis (which means that they must always be personally graded by the instructor and never by his assistant), there are nevertheless some things that can be done to assure fairness in grading. For instance, exams can be marked one question at a time so that whatever standards are used in grading are more likely to be consistently applied across all students. This method also prevents a single student from being the victim of the instructor's too severe initial standards or his fatigue at the conclusion of marking an entire batch of papers. Lastly, marking by question will prevent the instructor from observing the names on the paper and will assure that the mark is based on the paper's content rather than on the instructor's opinion about the student.

Since only a few essays can be asked for on any single examination, each will carry a lot of weight in grading, and since even the best of students may be unable to understand or answer an occasional question it follows that some choice of questions should be provided for on essay exams.

Objective questions, such as true or false or multiple

choice items, have just the opposite characteristics of essays. They are much more difficult to write and present a more formidable test production problem but they are easier to mark and can cover a much wider area of the course although with less depth. Since they are marked objectively your assistant can grade them as well as you, which will save time. They are much less fatiguing to students than essay questions are. This is another way of saying that they are somewhat easier. Also the irrelevant effect of writing skill on the part of the student is eliminated.

Do not confuse a short answer or fill-in test with an objective test. These are subjective and must be personally marked by the instructor, for no matter how carefully these questions are planned students will always come up with correct responses that were not anticipated.

Many textbooks come with an instructor's manual containing a collection of suggested test questions keyed to each chapter in the book. Often these questions are prepared by the author's graduate students and are of questionable quality. If you can pick and choose among them, you may be able to get a number of useful questions, particularly if you modify them or use them as a source of ideas. Ideally examination questions should be related to either the lectures or the text, preferably both. A good objective question should have at least four characteristics:

1. It should be clear and unambiguous.
2. It should have one and only one correct answer.
3. It should relate to some important aspect of the course.
4. It should be difficult enough so that an unprepared student will get it wrong but easy enough for a properly prepared student to get it right.

If you are going to use objective questions you ought to collect data on them over the years to see how well they meet the foregoing criteria. By retaining the better questions and discarding or modifying the poorer ones, you can develop a good question pool of your own that you can sample in creating new examinations. However, question items, like lecture notes, can become obsolete with time, and data on them must be kept current.

One effective way of evaluating objective questions is to do a frequency count of the number of times that the top students in a class get the question wrong. For example, if with a four-alternative multiple choice question you consider the top twelve papers, then it would be expected that if the question were totally unrelated to the course nine students would get it wrong and three would get it right purely on the basis of chance. What you then do is look at each question that approaches the chance value of nine out of twelve students getting it wrong, and consider if this question is fair within the context of your course. Notice that the frequency count does not make this decision for you; this is a matter of professional judgment. The count merely points out which questions require reevaluation. Sometimes the high error count will be because the question is inappropriate for the course as you taught it and sometimes it will be due to a defect in the question itself. This again is a matter for your professional judgment.

Notice that this type of question analysis will not only permit you to build up a pool of good quality items for future use, it will also give you a valid basis for adjusting class grades by discarding unreasonable questions. It will do one other useful thing for you. It will provide you with a conclusive answer for the student who claims that a particular question was ambiguous, tricky, or otherwise misleading or unfair since if the question was in fact a good one you can demonstrate to him that the other students were not affected by the defect that he claims the question to suffer from.

If an examination is to consist of a set of numerical problems to be solved, as is often the case in an engineering course, the instructor may want to consider the possibility of using an open book exam (one in which the students are permitted to bring whatever reference materials they choose to the examination). This makes it possible to give problems that require the use of detailed tables or graphs for their solution. An alternative to this is for the instructor to distribute any necessary reference materials as part of the examination. This may be a preferable method as it does not preclude the inclusion of short answer questions in the same test, as would be the case in an open book exam. It also prevents penalizing the student who has made a poor choice of reference material to bring with him, and it may even prevent a hernia or two among overly cautious students who would otherwise bring their entire library to the exam.

I had an instructor in engineering school who used to permit his classes to bring to his exams one standard sized index card containing any formulae that the students cared to jot down as a legal "crib sheet." It turned out that the students learned so much about the course in preparing these index cards that they usually weren't needed during the test. This policy also did much to eliminate problems with cribbing in the course, but probably had the undesirable side effect of ruining the eyesight of many of us prematurely in our efforts to read our own microwriting.

I do not favor the use of a surprise quiz as a method of forcing students to keep current in their studies, primarily because I am opposed to the idea of forcing students to study. This device only has to be used by an instructor who has failed to get the students interested enough to want to study the material and hence is really an admission of failure on the part of the instructor who resorts to it.

Students are entitled to at least a week's notice of an examination so that they can properly schedule their preparations. At the time of your announcing an exam, the students should also be given an idea of its format and content areas. If the class has never had a prior examination with you, consider presenting a sample of a few short answer type questions to give them some idea of how you think when selecting test items. After the first examination this is not necessary as the students will have had a good sampling of your propensities in writing exams.

It is also useful prior to an essay exam to give your class some idea of how to organize an answer properly. This will tend to help their grades as well as make your grading task a little easier. It is particularly important to instruct students on how to answer numerical problems in such a manner that you have some basis for the awarding of partial credit for an essentially correct technique that through a few minor errors produced an erroneous result. By the way, one of the major points to bear in mind when preparing a numerical problem is to design it in such a manner that intermediate computations are recorded. This will prevent an error in an early stage of the computation from resulting in a total loss of credit.

Most students realize that on an objective type test with no additional points deducted for wrong answers it is advantageous for them to guess. They also know that if they can eliminate one obviously wrong answer out of four they then have a one in three chance of getting the answer correct instead of only a one in four chance. What many students do not realize, however, unless you advise them on the matter, is that even if extra points are taken off papers for wrong answers it is still to their advantage to guess. For example, on a four-alternative multiple choice test if one correct answer is deducted for every three errors made this is not a penalty for guessing but an attempt to control for it.

The idea behind this scoring scheme is that if a student guessed on the basis of no knowledge at all at four questions he would by chance alone get three wrong and one correct. By deducting this one correct answer the scoring system seeks to eliminate the effect of guessing. In a true-false test the same result would be obtained by the deduction of one correct answer for each error made. The point, of course, is that under such a corrective method of scoring the student's score should be the same whether he guesses at answers or not assuming that his luck is about average. But remember that the foregoing is based on the assumption that the student has no knowledge at all concerning the question. If he has some partial knowledge such as the realization that one or more of the alternative answers is incorrect, then his probability of guessing the correct answer is better than the one chance in four that the correction scheme is based on and this type of intelligent guessing will improve his score. It may sound at first that by pointing out these considerations to your students you are teaching them how to get by in school with minimal effort, but this is not true. What you are in fact teaching them is how to get credit for whatever partial knowledge they may have. Their understanding of this principle will actually result in your test's being a more sensitive measure and will also enable your students to compete more effectively on the variety of selection instruments that they will be exposed to in the future course of their academic and professional careers.

Term papers are really a special type of essay examination for which the student is given an extended time to respond and he is not only permitted but usually required to consult reference sources. It is both a learning and a testing vehicle but primarily a learning device. It permits a much greater depth of treatment of the subject matter than is possible in a classroom examination. The fact that it can be typed is also a great aid to the instructor in evaluating it, but the evaluation must still be based on subjective criteria.

In preparing a term paper, the student usually learns a great deal about a restricted area. I tend to have a negative attitude toward term papers, having wasted a great deal of time writing them as a student and reading them as an instructor. The basic problem with term papers is that nobody ever wrote a good one unless he had something that he wanted to say and the condition precedent of having something to say is not created by being assigned a paper to write.

Perhaps the best way of dealing with term papers is to make them optional so that people who do want to write them have the opportunity to do so but students who have nothing to say are not compelled to say it in thirty or more pages. If a term paper is to be made available as an option for an extra grade, it is important to distinguish between students who really want to write one and students who feel that they have to because they have a poor average. These latter students would be better advised to spend more time in studying the material rather than wasting valuable study time preparing an optional paper.

If a term paper is to be optional, it should be made clear to the class that it is just that and that it is possible to get an A without writing a paper. Furthermore they should be told that submitting a poor one will not improve their mark. The ground rules for the format should be made clear at the beginning including such matters as the deadline for the submission of papers and the requirement that they be typed.

I usually advise against the submission of a paper unless the student really wants to do it, and make it a practice to tell a class that I regard my obligation as being limited to reading the first five pages of any paper submitted. If the students want me to read beyond that point they have five pages to convince me that it's worth my time to do so.

You should always require that the topic and a preliminary outline be approved by you in advance to assure that the topic selected and the approach taken is worthwhile and is neither too broad nor too restrictive to be properly handled. You should also make it clear that you are available for consultation and guidance if the student requires it.

It is unreasonable and unfair not to advise students beforehand of your grading criteria for papers. It must be emphasized that quality is more important than quantity and that a shorter but adequate paper is more impressive than a longer one that is incoherent and disorganized.

In some courses, oral reports are utilized. These can be valuable in giving students experience in public speaking, which is a useful skill *per se,* but student talks have to be used with caution as poor quality presentations tend to destroy class interest. There are two ways to minimize this drawback. One is to keep student presentations brief and interspaced with other material. Another is to give a lecture or two on how to prepare and deliver good oral reports. Probably the greatest source of difficulty with student talks is that the student is so concerned with impressing the instructor that he is completely oblivious to his real audience, the class. To minimize this problem it is a good idea not to grade students on these presentations and to be sure that this policy is understood by all speakers.

No matter what type of examination you give to a class, you will always get reactions of nervousness and distraction which will prevent some students from following the simplest of instructions. A calm, reassuring manner on your part will do much to minimize this and increase the validity of the test results.

Some instructors become so obsessed with eliminating cheating by closely proctoring examinations that their behavior becomes insulting to the vast majority of students who are not attempting to cheat. This is a foolish, shortsighted type of behavior on the part of the instructor, who is jeopardizing a relationship with a class that he may have spent half a term in developing to prevent one or two students from cheating.

There are some basic facts about cribbing that an instructor ought to be aware of. In the first place it is not possible to prevent every possible case of cheating on an exam. In the second place it is not important to do so. The one or two questions that a dishonest student may steal the answer to will rarely affect his mark significantly. Thirdly, your relationship with the majority of the class who are not cheating is vastly more important than stopping the occasional cheater. For these reasons you ought to give serious consideration to conducting your exams on the honor system.

If, on the other hand, you feel that you cannot permit this type of activity to go undetected, you should at least be sure not to involve the rest of the class in this embarrassing situation. The offender should be talked to privately and then only in those situations where there is conclusive evidence that he is in fact guilty of cheating. You ought to be extremely reluctant to pursue this matter beyond an initial talking to the student unless there is clear and convincing evidence that this was not an isolated incident and the student is continuing in this course of conduct. Any doubt should be resolved in favor of the student's innocence.

After you have collected a group of marks for each student in the class, the problem that remains is how to convert them into a final grade. The basic approach is to compute an average and translate this mechanically into a letter grade, but this scheme may require certain modifications to allow for special circumstances. For example, how do you handle the situation where a student has missed an exam during the term?

One way of handling this problem is to have make-up exams available for students who missed an exam for a good reason. This will require that you make up twice the number of examinations that you would normally require and is not in general a sound policy, except in special circumstances, such as when a student through no fault of his own missed several exams and there is no other basis to assign him a mark. The free availability of make-up exams will encourage students to miss examinations for unacceptable reasons such as not feeling that they are ready for it. In effect, it will cause some students to consider the regular examinations as optional.

Another approach is to give the student who missed an exam for a valid reason an average based on the examinations that he took while giving a zero to the student who willfully missed an exam. There are two problems with this approach. In the first place, it motivates students to lie about their reason for missing an exam, and in the second place, the penalty is so severe that it is difficult to enforce it. It is also unfair to the student whose grade is based on a full set of test scores. Whatever system you decide on, the class should be informed of it in advance and it ought to be flexible enough so that you are not precluded from using common sense in enforcing it.

In some cases you might want to drop the lowest mark that a student gets during the term in recognition of the fact that everyone has an occasional bad day and in an effort to give him the best possible grade. This practice removes some of the inequities inherent in having some students' averages based on different numbers of tests than others' and it can reduce student anxiety about exams, but it can create other problems. For example, if you drop the lowest test score it may become possible for a student to get a higher grade than another who has a higher overall average depending on how individual test scores are distributed. Hence if you plan to use this type of grading method you can't promise your class in advance that you will be able to do so without imposing the condition that it must not result in any such inequities.

You must always be careful about what promises you make to a class concerning grading procedures because having made the commitment you must scrupulously observe it no matter how many unforeseen problems are created.

Even if you have done a question analysis and adjustment on each test during the term you may still have to make some adjustment in the final grades. A fairly straightforward way of doing this is to assume that there should be a certain percentage of A's in the course and to add a sufficient number of points to each average to produce this percentage of A's. The remaining distribution of marks will then be determined. This method can also be used to adjust essay test scores where the type of question analysis previously mentioned can't be utilized. The only remaining problem will be the making of decisions concerning those individual students who fall close to the dividing point between two grades. Here such factors as attendance record, grade trends, and class participation may be considered.

The basis of all adjustments and grading decisions must be individual for each course and should be recorded in your roll book for future reference. As far as possible, grades should be computed from test scores without knowledge of which scores belong to which students unless subjective factors must be taken into account in a particular course.

There are a large number of possible grading schemes. A good one ought to have at least the following characteristics:

1. It should be based on an adequate sampling.
2. It should be equitable and fairly applied.
3. It should be consistent but not so inflexible that special circumstances can't be handled.
4. The students should be informed of it at the beginning of the term.

10.
The Selection of Texts and Materials

There are two common, troublesome situations that an instructor will often find himself in with regard to the choice of a suitable textbook for a course. Either there may be so many suitable books available that it is difficult to choose among them or an adequate text for the course in question is not in print.

The first situation is the easier to deal with, for often the conflict can be resolved by a systematic consideration of the essential factors in textbook selection. Ideally a text should be selected by both the instructor and the student with each party evaluating a different aspect of the selection criteria.

The major contribution to the selection process that must be made by the instructor is the evaluation of the text with respect to its coverage of the required material, its accuracy and currency, and the appropriateness of its depth of coverage. The major difficulty that most instructors have with this evaluation process will usually be in finding the time to adequately review the large number of potential texts. This situation is usually compounded by the fact that even old, familiar works require reevaluation when new editions come out, and often book salesmen who supply examination copies of texts to be considered for adoption fail to supply them early enough for an adequate review.

Unfortunately, the major reason for a revised edition often is to prevent students from buying used copies. I have had to discontinue the use of one excellent text because the revised edition destroyed the book and the original edition could no longer be obtained. There would seem to be a real ethical issue involved with texts that are constantly revised. If the revisions represent substantial improvements or up-datings this is a positive factor. If they leave the book essentially unchanged and are merely designed to increase sales then the professor has an obligation to his students not to specify such a text if there is a satisfactory alternative available. An examination copy of a book is for the purpose of your evaluating it for possible class adoption. It is not a bribe, and it does not transfer your obligation from your students to the publisher supplying it.

Besides the technical adequacy of the book, the instructor must also evaluate how effectively a text will fit into his particular course. There must be a reasonable amount of overlap between a text and your lectures, but they should not follow each other too closely. Ideally, the text and the lectures should supplement each other in such a manner that the student is provided with a somewhat different emphasis or viewpoint by each. Points that the student may find unclear in the lecture may then be clarified by the text and vice versa. It is for this reason that you should not use the same text in your course that you used as a student. If you do, you may find that your lecture notes follow the text too closely and the two don't provide a needed contrast. This also speaks against the common practice of an instructor's specifying a text that he has written, unless it is used as a supplement to another book or is really the only suitable one available.

You will probably never find a text that covers the material in exactly the same order that your lectures do unless you write it yourself, but this is not a particularly crucial matter. There are two ways of handling this situation. Either provide a course syllabus keying the text chapters to the lectures or advise the students to read the text in the order in which it is written, which is how the author intended it to be read, and leave it to the students to ultimately integrate the lectures with the text. The latter method is probably the more effective but the choice may be left to the personal preference of the individual student.

The role of the student in textbook evaluation is in the area of deciding how interesting and understandable the work is. You as an expert may find a particular text both fascinating and scholarly, but unless your students find it helpful and readable it is totally useless. No student ever learned anything from a book that he didn't read. The first time that you use a new text about the best you can do is to make an educated guess as to how students will react to it. An attractive format and adequate illustrations and artwork may be important considerations in this regard. In recent years there has been a noticeable preoccupation on the part of publishers with such factors and this is probably a healthy development. At the conclusion of the course you should always solicit student comments on the text. If they like it as much as you do you have a winner and you should stay with it until something better comes along or until the book begins to become obsolete. On the other hand, if student reaction to a text is adverse, replace it the next time you teach the course. There are enough problems in teaching without handicapping yourself with an ineffective text.

If several texts differ in quality then the choice should be based on this factor. In the situation where there appears to be little variation in quality among several potential choices then the decision may have to be based on secondary factors.

Many texts are accompanied by an instructor's manual giving suggestions for the effective use of the book and a pool of potential test items based on it. There may also be a student work manual that is coordinated with the text. These can be valuable if well prepared, particularly to a beginning instructor. When you request examination copies of books, always be sure to inquire about the existence of these aids and ask that they be sent along with the text.

Another important consideration in textbook selection is the price of the book. If all other factors are equal you ought to consider your students' financial situation and specify the least expensive book.

It is neither fair nor desirable to request a desk copy of a book from the publisher every time that you use it in a course, but it is helpful to have at least two copies of texts that you use often and keep one in your office and one at home. In this way the book will always be available in whichever place you happen to be working. One copy will invariably be at the wrong location when you need it. Whenever you order a book for a course that you have previously used you should always request your secretary to ask the publisher for a desk copy in the event that they have changed the edition since the last time the book was used. Otherwise, the first notice you may get of this change is likely to be at the beginning of the term, when you may find yourself the only one in the class without a copy of the textbook. This is not a good position for any instructor to find himself in.

In the more difficult circumstances where there is no text that you consider adequate for your course, there are certain alternatives open to you. In the first place there is no law that requires every course to have a text. If the reason that a suitable textbook can't be found is that the course is a highly specialized one, it may be possible to eliminate the need for a text by distributing a set of handout materials or a list of library references, or both. Even if a text is available it may be desirable to supplement it with this type of material.

The problem with library references is that they tend to consume an undue amount of the student's time and library facilities will be overloaded rapidly if they are used as a substitute for a textbook. This is the reason for the publication of readings collections. If a good readings book is available that meets the requirements of your course, it can provide your students with all of the advantages of a good reference list without the physical inconvenience of having to constantly be in and out of the library. The problem, of course, is that nobody will ever write a readings book that you think is perfect unless you do it yourself, so unless you consider doing just that you may still desire to give out a supplementary readings list. The availability of a readings book will permit this supplementary reference list to be much briefer.

If you do decide to prepare your own readings collection and if your collection is not likely to be of interest to a sufficient number of other instructors it might be difficult to get it published. If your course enrollment is large enough there are firms that will prepare special reading collections for you if guaranteed some minimum number of sales. These tend to be unduly expensive for the students unless you have substantial numbers of them and I have seen some collections where the physical reproduction could only be described as horrendous. Also some publishers will limit your selection of items not originally published by them. Possibly a better alternative is the specifying of a collection of reprints that some publishers will supply in kit form at a reasonable cost. No matter what form your reading assignments take, always be selective about what you ask your students to read. A collection of poorly written articles is usually effective in destroying student interest.

The most common solution to the problem of there being no adequate text available is to specify two or more texts which will collectively cover the required material. This requires you to become especially conscious of the costs involved to the students as you will find that student enrollment in elective courses will begin to fall off when text costs begin to approach tuition expenses.

The reader may be inclined to believe that if there is no adequate single text available for his course it might be a good idea for him to write one on the theory that not only would this solve his selection problem but also there might be a good market for such a book. This may prove to be true, but if nobody has written a particular book it may pay you to first consider if there isn't some reason for this situation. For example, I have for many years been unable to find a single textbook that would adequately cover the material presented in my physiological psychology course. I suspect that the reason that such a book has never been written is that it would require such an expensive staff of medical illustrators, photographers, and draftsmen that the market does not justify the expenses of publication.

Often trade or government publications will make good relatively inexpensive texts in specialized areas. A military standard has proven to be one of the best books available for my human engineering course.

If a good text isn't available for a course this simply means that the role of the instructor becomes more important than ever. If the students can't follow him they have no place else to turn.

It is rarely justifiable to specify purely reference works for a course, but students in a particular program would be well advised to gradually acquire a set of basic ones that they are likely to use over and over in several courses. For example, every law student will need a good law dictionary early in his career and most engineering students will find a few basic handbooks in their specialties valuable.

As in the case of reference books the instructor will often want to recommend additional books to the class which are not required reading but which will prove helpful if the student wants to explore the subject in greater depth. Thus in a real sense an instructor has to be something of a book critic to be effective in guiding his students' studies. If he recommends dull material his suggestions won't be followed the second time. If he selects ineffective material he is wasting his class's time and defeating his own purpose.

When students are required to purchase special instruments such as slide rules, dissection kits, microscopes, and so forth for use in their course of study, the particular devices or an acceptable group to choose from should be specified by the school since at the time of the initial purchase most students are ignorant of the important selection factors to be considered. If left to their own resources they will often waste considerable sums of money on equipment which will prove unserviceable and ultimately have to be replaced.

In addition to specialized equipment practically every student today will need a good serviceable electric typewriter and many will require some type of calculator. It would be helpful if college catalogues gave students some guidelines as to what to look for when purchasing these items.

There has been an increasing tendency in recent years for students to take advantage of the electronic age by bringing portable cassette recorders to class and asking the instructor's permission to tape the lecture. This may permit the student to obtain a record of every gem of wisdom emitted by even the fastest lecturer, but the practice presents enough difficulties to justify discouraging it, if not actually prohibiting it. For one thing it tends to prevent the student from acquiring efficient note taking and organizing skills. In spite of appearances it doesn't really save him any effort. Actually it forces him to sit through the lecture again when he transcribes it at home, only this time he must do so in the absence of any material written on the board and without the opportunity to ask questions.

The two major objections to this practice are that it tends to make the student unduly passive and inactive during the lecture and it also tends to inhibit the spontaneity of the lecturer who knows that every offhand comment he makes is being recorded. Unless the instructor makes a conscientious effort to forget about the presence of the recorder the lecture that his class receives may suffer substantially. Even I, who like to consider myself as fairly candid, have been known to temper my remarks concerning prominent political figures in the presence of a functioning tape recorder.

As advances in modern technology bring more and more sophisticated business equipment such as copiers and programable calculators into the price range of individual consumers there is no reason why future generations of both teachers and students should not avail themselves of such devices to reduce the amount of time wasted on purely clerical procedures and to allow more time to be spent on the business of thinking and evaluating, the prime functions of students and academicians.

11.
Evaluating and Improving Your Teaching

The evaluation of current performance is a necessary prerequisite to improving any professional skill. Unless an instructor has a reasonably accurate understanding of his own strengths and weaknesses, it is not possible for him to direct his efforts at professional improvement to those areas where they are most needed. The adoption of new methods and techniques merely for the sake of their novelty or because they work well for someone else is just as likely to detract from a teacher's effectiveness as it is to enhance it unless these new methods are adopted with the specific goal of remedying known deficiencies or weaknesses in the instructor's professional work.

Conversely, the self-evaluation of an instructor's job performance will prove a total waste of time unless the results of such self-evaluation are utilized for continuing professional growth. The first question that must be considered in this chapter relates to what vehicles there are available to the instructor to aid him in achieving an accurate self-evaluation.

The major sources of such information that will be discussed are:

1. Student opinion surveys

2. Informal student feedback, direct and indirect
3. Evaluations by peers and supervisors
4. Performance of students
5. Recorded lectures.

Formal surveys of student opinion concerning instructors are probably the most common method of faculty evaluation used. These questionnaires may be distributed by the department in question or by the university to aid it in making personnel decisions on such matters as promotions, rehire, or tenure and the results may be reported to the individual faculty member to provide him with feedback on his performance. Such surveys may also be distributed by faculty members on their own initiative. If your university does not use such questionnaires or if you don't believe that the form being used is optimal you should develop your own form and use it to provide you with the additional information that you require.

If your school is proposing the use of such forms you should support the idea even if it is proposed to publish the results publicly. If universities do not attempt to measure teaching ability by whatever methods are available to them how is high quality teaching ever to be recognized and rewarded and how are teaching standards to be upgraded? An unfavorable rating may be painful and embarrassing to a faculty member, but the same may be said about a student's reaction to a poor grade. If the faculty member in question is genuinely concerned about his performance, this information will ultimately benefit him. If he is not concerned about it, there is little reason to feel much sympathy for him. There are many well-paying jobs where the great American standard of mediocrity is perfectly acceptable. College teaching isn't one of them.

Figures 3 and 4 in the appendix show two samples of student course rating forms that have been used by different instructors, but for best results you ought to design your own to meet your personalized requirements. A lot of thought should go into this design as once you use a form for a period of time you will be reluctant to make changes due to the amount of data that you will have acquired about the form and its interpretation.

As is the case with any opinion survey there are two approaches that can be taken in designing the instrument. You can either provide fixed alternative responses or request an open ended response where the respondent is requested to write out an answer to the questions asked.

Fixed alternative responses are quicker and easier for the students to make. They may take the form of a rating scale or a letter grade as in the samples given. You must be careful with fixed alternatives to provide for any response that a student might want to make. You must also be careful to assure that students read the instructions carefully; otherwise the instrument might be filled out exactly opposite to what they intended. This source of error can often be detected if you combine a fixed alternative questionnaire with an opportunity at the end for any additional free responses that the student cares to make. This is done in the two sample instruments.

Such a combination of formats makes it possible to get a rapid survey of student opinion on the fixed alternative items while permitting students who feel strongly enough to make the more onerous personal responses to do so. This is particularly useful in the case of a student who wants to comment on areas not covered in the fixed alternative portion or who desires to elaborate on his answer. These free responses will prove the most valuable. Many of them will be treasured by you for years, and unless you have too thick a skin to be an effective teacher, some of them may leave deep burning scars. Obviously, if you are to get any useful information from a student survey it must be taken anonymously. The contemptible practice of analyzing handwriting to find out who wrote all those terrible things about you will be betrayed by your manner toward the student in question and will rapidly result in your getting back a series of bland, worthless class ratings in future classes. If students learn that they cannot rely on your assurances of anonymity they also learn that they cannot rely on you for anything else, and your effectiveness with them will be zero.

In addition to deciding on the form of the questionnaire, you must consider the content areas to be sampled. As a minimum you should seek information about student attitudes toward the instructor's personality and teaching ability, his tests and fairness in grading them, how interesting or dull the course was, and what effect if any it may have had on the students' future academic careers. This is also a good opportunity to get student views on the texts used and to solicit their suggestions as to what if anything should be changed, added, or deleted to improve the course.

However much care may be expended in the preparation of a survey form, the quality of the information that it obtains will be limited by the amount of care with which the students respond to it and which the instructor employs in its analysis.

A convenient way to summarize the results of a class survey is to make a frequency count of the number of times each scale position is checked off for each question on the fixed alternative items and to compute an average rating. Occasionally you will notice inconsistent responses on a particular questionnaire, such as the student who says that your lectures are always dull and confusing, your personality is always unpleasant and your knowledge of your material is minimal and who then goes on to rate you as an excellent teacher. Unless this inconsistency is explained in the open ended responses it probably results from the careless reading of the questionnaire. To eliminate problems with carelessly filled out forms by people who really don't want to make any comments but feel compelled to, it is a good plan to make the submission of the questionnaire optional and to say that it is only for those students who are willing to make the effort to respond carefully.

The best way of summarizing open end responses is to

categorize the statements made into as many different categories as is necessary and to do a frequency count on each substantive comment made.

Student rating forms, while useful, are not panaceas. They are most valuable for confirming the subjective feelings that the instructor himself has concerning a course.

All student surveys are subject to having their accuracy lowered by halo effects. A halo effect is the tendency of students to give better ratings on all scales to instructors whom they like and lower ratings to professors that they do not like regardless of the scale's irrelevance to the factor of likeability. Therefore the instructor's score on scales that deal with his personality are an important index of the likelihood of there being a substantial halo effect present.

Sometimes it is useful to ask students about objective matters that the instructor himself is capable of evaluating accurately in addition to matters touching on his professional abilities that are more difficult for him to objectively assess. This will permit him to gauge the accuracy of the students' responses to the more subjective items, using their responses to the objective ones as a calibration standard. The item on one of the sample questionnaires inquiring about the amount of class participation in the course is such an item, but unfortunately in this particular form it suffers from a certain amount of ambiguity and about half of the students responding to it treat it as though what was being asked was not the factual matter of how much class participation there was but how desirable the amount obtained was. Hence, in a given class answers to this item tend to be bimodal. This is the type of defect in a form that must be guarded against in its design.

The most effective use of student surveys will result from the keeping of cumulative records of performance in each course from term to term and noting the development of trends.

In the course of his day-to-day interaction with students the instructor will usually get a certain amount of feedback concerning the strong and weak points of his courses. While this type of personal student comment is likely to be more inhibited as it is not made anonymously but on a face-to-face basis, nevertheless, in those cases where there is a good rapport between the student and the instructor, the student may feel secure enough to express his views with a good deal of candor. This source of student reaction is particularly valuable because unlike the situation with a student opinion survey the instructor is in a position to follow up on the students' reactions by asking questions to clarify his views or to get him to elaborate on them. It also has the advantage of permitting the instructor to know and thereby be in a position to evaluate the source of the comment. The instructor can ask himself if the student has some motive to serve by his comments other than to inform the instructor of a problem or of a job well done. He may also evaluate how capable the student is to observe and report the situation accurately.

Student comments may be offered spontaneously or may be solicited by the instructor, but solicitation should be used with care and it is not to be recommended (except in the most general way) unless the instructor is concerned about some specific problem that he believes to exist with his course. The danger is that such questions may embarrass students and discourage personal communications with the instructor when such communications are needed.

No one student comment, no matter how reliable the source, can be considered as conclusive about any situation, but when several students independently make the same comment it ought to be taken seriously and the matter should be investigated.

Often comments about an instructor will be made to other instructors and over a period of time everybody in a department will acquire some sort of a reputation among both his colleagues and the students as either a good teacher or one to avoid if possible. This type of reputation may be important, but it is usually not specific enough to be of much value in correcting performance defects even when specific student comments are relayed to the instructor secondhand by colleagues.

It is important for the instructor to avoid discussing the shortcomings of his colleagues with students or even giving them the impression that he believes that their complaints are justified. There are usually at least two sides to every story and in this situation the instructor being consulted has only heard one. This is not to say that a student who appears to have a legitimate complaint should not be advised as to how to pursue it if it can't be satisfactorily resolved by a conference with the instructor complained of. It also does not preclude the instructor from discussing the situation with the instructor complained of or from even offering him advice on the situation provided that the personal relationship between the two people involved warrants it, and it will not involve violating any of the student's confidences. This type of consultation should never be made unless at the student's request or with his express permission, as in this case the student communication is clearly intended to be confidential in the absence of an express statement to the contrary.

The evaluative comments concerning an instructor made by colleagues performing personnel committee functions or the department chairman in making periodic evaluations are often required to be communicated to him and may range in value from great to negligible. If these comments are the result of adequate observation and consideration by competent people trying hard to do a good job then they are valuable. If they are based on inadequate information or departmental politics they are worthless.

Often the evaluations of department chairmen tend to be either bland or invariable across the entire department. This results from a department chairman's abdicating his function of evaluating the faculty. He simply makes general comments because he is required to say something and he wishes to minimize controversy. While nonevaluative "evaluations" like this may be worthless with respect to improving instructor performance, they can be quite valuable in alerting the better professors that there is no future for them in a department run by such a person and that they ought to start looking for other professional opportunities.

Since it is not possible for any person to be either perfect or a complete incompetent, it follows that the more specific the comment made the more useful it is. Comments on an instructor's teaching abilities made by a first rate teacher are worthy of great weight. Comments made by people who are themselves inept or indifferent teachers regardless of their prominence in other fields of endeavor are entitled to little consideration. As in the case of student feedback the quality of faculty comment is a function of the motivation behind the comment and the opportunity and ability to make sound observations.

A good index of instructor performance is student performance. If an instructor's students do well not only in his courses but in subsequent work that these courses form the foundation for, if they get into and do well in the graduate or professional schools of their choice, then it suggests that the instructor must be doing something right. Of course they may achieve this success not because of the instructor but in spite of him. Therefore student performance in the instructor's own courses or the immediately following ones is the most significant performance to look at as here the instructor's effect will be maximal. If students don't do well in an instructor's course, taking into account both the grading standards that he employs and an allowance for student variability, this will suggest the presence of one or more problems that require identification and correction.

The tape recording of an occasional lecture gives an instructor a chance to hear himself as a student hears him. This technique can be quite revealing at times. For example, I was completely unaware of how often I used the expression "now" as an introductory exclamation to preface new material. Such a recording will give an instructor a good idea of his style of delivery and class personality. This type of information can be obtained in no other way.

All of the foregoing methods of self-evaluation have certain advantages and limitations, but more than this they each tend to focus on a different aspect of professorial job performance. Hence the most effective self-evaluation is made by using as many of these devices and others as possible. This will permit you to get a total integrated picture of your own strong and weak points. An instructor with such knowledge is in a position to seek improvement in areas where it is needed and can work toward this goal effectively.

In rare situations there may be a conflict between the results obtained from these different methods of evaluation. This will require a careful analysis on the part of the instructor to determine the reasons for the contradiction and which result is likely to be the more accurate. Most apparent conflicts in results, however, will prove on reflection not to be true conflicts, but to result from the complexity of the subject matter being measured. There is no such dichotomy as a good or a bad teacher. Each of us is a combination of many specific abilities and skills. We may rate high on some factors, low on others, and intermediate on still others. The fact that an instructor is rated as a good lecturer and a poor discussion leader does not indicate a conflict in evaluation; it simply describes the way he is. It is only if one source rates a professor as a good lecturer and another source rates him poor on the same criterion that a conflict exists.

Having discovered the areas in which improvement is needed, the instructor must next ask how this improvement can be attained. One source of new ideas or new viewpoints concerning old ideas can be provided by books such as this one which should be sought out and perused. Unfortunately there are not too many available that are directed toward the problems of college as opposed to high school or grammar school teaching. This probably results from the fact that college teaching is not really regarded as highly in academic circles as most college administrators like to say it is, and a good practical work on the possibility of obtaining instrumental conditioning in a planarian is likely to provide a potential author with far more enhancement of his chances for professional advancement and prestige than a book on college teaching. Nevertheless such books are worth the effort to find, for if their authors believe strongly enough that they have something to say that is worth such a quixotic effort, it is likely that the reader will be able to pick up a few useful ideas from them.

Soliciting the opinions of your colleagues, particularly the better teachers among them, on how to deal with specific problems can be productive. Not only will you get many valuable ideas in this manner but your inquiry is generally quite flattering and will in and of itself do much to further pleasant and productive interpersonal relationships with your colleagues. No matter how good you may be in your work there is always something you can learn from others that can make you even better, and the other person involved need not necessarily be a better or more experienced teacher than yourself. He doesn't even have to be as good.

Unquestionably the most productive source of improvement is the studying of the methods of other teachers, both the good and the not-so-good. This need not be limited to a retrospective consideration of your own professors in college or graduate school. Every time you attend a lecture or a seminar at some professional society you should get into the habit of studying the lecturer as well as his material.

There is no reason why you should not ask a colleague for permission to sit in on one of his classes to see how he handles a certain type of problem, particularly if he has given you advice on the matter in question.

If you get into the habit of noticing the unique teaching styles of others, you cannot help but be amazed at how effectively some people can utilize the most diverse or unorthodox teaching methods. The reader, when considering how effectively he might be able to adopt what appears to be some far out teaching methodology, must be careful to distinguish between a well-planned, effective utilization of a particular instructor's personality and mere eccentric behavior. Also the rare individual who can use sarcasm and other terror course techniques to activate students and still manage to stop short of offending them and destroying a working rapport with a class, must be sharply distinguished from the average professor who resorts to such practices as the result of having bad manners rather than any remarkable teaching skill. It is somewhat appalling how often this situation is perceived by such a person's colleagues as reflecting the high standards that he sets for student performance. Nothing could be further from the truth. What this type of behavior really indicates is a total lack of regard for student development.

The beginning instructor would do well to avoid experimenting with any extreme type of behavior in a classroom until he is sufficiently skilled to be able to accurately and rapidly evaluate its effect on his class.

One thing that every professor should do from time to time is to enroll in a course as a student, not primarily for the sake of the course material or even to study the techniques of the instructor but to keep alive and vivid his memory of what it is like to be a student and what problems students have. Too many of us tend to forget this with the passage of the years and this is one of the few things that are vital for a teacher never to forget.

To really remember what it is like to be a student it is necessary not just to audit a course but to take it for credit so that you must prepare for and take examinations. Whenever possible this should be done at another institution or in a department where you are not known. Few professors who remember their own student days and how traumatic they were at times will fail to have the kind of empathy and understanding of students that good student-teacher rapport must be based on.

Any real improvement or maintenance of high teaching standards must be based on the motivation supplied by the professor's conviction that his students and his profession are of prime importance to him. With this attitude you are practically assured of success as a teacher. Without it, even if you possess special gifts you have two strikes against you.

12.
Faculty Interrelationships and Politics

People find their way into academic careers for a large variety of reasons. Some may enter the field as a result of their admiration for one or more former professors and the desire to emulate them. Others may enter the field because it seemed like fun (which it is) or the amount of free time that they thought instructors had (which they don't) was attractive, or just for lack of any better opportunities. Still others enter to fulfill a need for power and dominance or personal aggrandizement and prestige. People even enter the field as I did, more or less by accident.

With the average college faculty made up of such a diverse group of people having such a variety of motivations it would be strange indeed if academic departments were not subject to much controversy and political manipulations.

As every psychologist worth his shingle knows, the closer and the more intimate a relationship between people the greater the opportunity for conflicts to arise between them. This is one of the reasons why intradepartmental feuding and politicking tends to be much more rancorous and bitter at times than interdepartmental conflicts or universitywide politics. Another reason for this regrettable state of affairs is that

117

unless the institution involved is a law school, most of the participants in departmental politics are really amateurs in the area of controversy and persuasion and often they do not have the same sense of restraint or propriety that the professional has. Thus, faculty politics can often be conducted on a quite personal basis and this can be destructive enough to effectively cripple a department or even an entire institution.

The beginning teacher, or for that matter even the more experienced one, who is primarily concerned with the business of being a teacher will doubtlessly be anxious to avoid this whole distasteful area. Unfortunately it is not possible for a professor to avoid involvement in the affairs of his department for a variety of reasons. Many of the decisions that are the subject of political controversy in a department will directly affect the day-to-day functioning of a professor and his ability to exercise his own professional judgment in relation to his work. They may also affect his financial security and advancement. Furthermore, a person has a real stake in the success and the development of the department in which he works and has an obligation to try to assure that it develops in the manner that he believes will make it more effective in servicing the needs of its students.

You will rapidly discover, should you actively seek to avoid any kind of political involvement, that the people involved in it will automatically take the view that "if you are not with us, you are against us" and you will find yourself involved anyway. The advice that Polonius gave to his son, to be slow to enter a controversy but once involved to conduct himself effectively, is still sound.

In fairness to academia it must be pointed out that the kind of political maneuvering that occurs on college campuses is no different in nature or intensity from the kind that occurs in industry or in any other organization made up of people. Political activity is not a characteristic of faculty members; it is a characteristic of people.

The primary purpose of this book is to help the reader

deal effectively with his students as opposed to training him as a politician. Nevertheless, having pointed out the reasons why a teacher must sometimes be politically effective, it is necessary to consider some of the factors involved in successfully advocating a position.

The basis of all effective political activity is the simple fact that all contested issues are ultimately decided either on the basis of a majority vote at a meeting or by the decision of a single person having the authority to make the decision. This basic fact and its implications are often lost sight of by amateur campus politicians. The real significance of this is that it implies that the amount of power you actually have in your department or university is directly related to your ability to persuade people. This in turn is directly related to how much respect the people that you attempt to persuade have for your judgment and integrity. This is the reason why personal abuse and threats are such counterproductive political techniques. They do not persuade the recipient but cause his position to harden because they lower his respect for the perpetrators of such tactics. The same is true with respect to the use of students as political pawns as is all too common in some contested tenure proceedings.

As a result of the fact that most departmental decisions are made by a majority vote, cliques of faculty members who think alike and tend to vote together across many different issues tend to develop. This creates a situation analogous to a political party and has the effect of enhancing this group's political power within a department by enabling it to present a solid block of votes on any issue. This in and of itself is a perfectly legitimate and proper activity. However, it provides the potential for a department to be divided into two warring factions who may be unable to agree on any necessary action or to work out acceptable compromises. This situation can effectively destroy any organization. Of course this type of stalemate will not occur if one clique has enough votes to assure a majority. The potential danger of this situation is realized if such a clique attempts to introduce political considerations into matters such as tenure deliberations or faculty retentions in an effort to increase its voting power. Such a practice is to be severely condemned not just because it is unfair to a candidate for tenure who may have devoted six years of his professional life to the institution, but even more importantly because if followed it will totally destroy the effectiveness of a department by loading it up with ineffective people who either have acceptable political views or are too craven or devious to express their opinions without the protective cloak of tenure.

If you personally vote at tenure committee meetings to retain political allies and to fire political adversaries rather than to retain good teachers and to release poor ones, your colleagues on both sides of the political fence will readily recognize this type of contemptible conduct for what it really is and both their respect for you and your influence with them will be sharply reduced. If your adversaries in departmental political wars use this type of tactic, fighting it out on the same basis will only harm both you and your cause. Retaining control of a department is less important than retaining your own self-respect.

This is not to imply that you cannot oppose an unsuitable candidate for tenure or rehire who incidentally happens to disagree with you on many departmental issues. What is important is that your decision be made on the merits of the case rather than on personal considerations.

As a practical matter the reader is more likely to be in the position of not having tenure, and of being concerned with how not to lose support for his tenure candidacy (as a result of being caught in the middle of a departmental squabble) than he is to be wondering how to vote at a tenure committee meeting.

My advice to such a faculty member is to conduct himself in such situations as if he had tenure. He must decide if the merits of the debate require his participation and if so which side he believes should be supported. If the honest and vigorous expression of his opinion concerning a departmental matter results in his not getting tenure, then before he condemns me for having given him bad advice he might reflect as to whether a thank you letter might not be in order for preventing him from wasting any more time in a department that has no future.

Incidentally, it is not really likely that the political group opposed by a nontenured faculty member has enough power to deny him tenure anyway, as if it had that clear-cut a majority it would simply run the department and there would be little controversy in such an organization. At least this will be the case until the ruling clique ultimately splits up into smaller cliques, which will usually happen when such a group gets too large to be effectively controlled by its leader.

I have long held the somewhat unpopular view in academic circles that the concept and practice of granting tenure has a greater potential for harming a teacher than for benefiting him. The theory behind the granting of tenure is that academic freedom is essential for the successful performance of a teacher's function and thus he must be protected from any pressures being exerted on him that might inhibit his free expression of ideas. Thus, after he has proven his ability and character for a required number of years he is cloaked with this immunity from arbitrary dismissal. It is hard to disagree with this basic theory, although its implicit assumption that somehow freedom of speech and expression is less important to people in fields other than teaching is not so easy to accept.

The real problem with tenure is that, as noted above, it does not protect freedom of speech among faculty members but actually inhibits it. The untenured faculty member is often intimidated in his freedom of action for a period of six years by the prospect of having to be approved for tenure by the very people whose ideas he may oppose. There can be no academic freedom for a faculty member whose self-interest clearly lies in avoiding offending people who have a life and death power over his professional career.

A second deleterious effect of tenure is the requirement that if it is not granted the candidate must be dismissed. If it were not for such a requirement, of course, a second class faculty who were never in a position to exercise free speech would be created by simply postponing tenure decisions. On the other hand this policy may result in the firing of many excellent teachers simply because the institution at which they are employed does not have a secure enough financial position to be sure that it will really require their services far into the future and it does not want to find itself in the difficult position of trying to dismiss tenured faculty for lack of work.

If a department is fully tenured it may make the infusion of new ideas into the department difficult or even impossible and the fear of this eventuality can also prevent the retention of worthy candidates whose only fault is that they did not inquire into the ratio of tenured to untenured faculty before they accepted a position.

The view is often expressed that mistakes in granting tenure cannot be remedied and that the system may require the retention of senile or incompetent faculty. In an effort to mitigate such effects of tenure most universities have adopted fairly early mandatory retirement ages. This is a classic case of the cure being worse than the disease, and this deleterious situation is an indirect effect of tenure.

Some people may be intellectually nonproductive at forty but many more function effectively into extreme old age. The setting of arbitrary and mandatory retirement ages without regard to the circumstance of the individual cases involved results in a loss of the talents of many of the most productive and experienced faculty members. Society does not have enough of such human resources to be able to throw them on the scrap heap prematurely without ultimately paying a price for this shortsighted behavior. Getting rid of an occasional tenured incompetent by forcing all faculty members to retire early regardless of how many useful years they may still have ahead of them is about as sensible as it is to burn down a house to get rid of termites.

From the foregoing the reader may get the impression that I am opposed to controversy and debate in academic departments. Actually nothing could be further from the truth. Our entire American legal system is based on adversary proceedings and it works extremely well. Vigorous advocacy of divergent points of view is one of the best ways of arriving at sound decisions in democratic institutions and is to be encouraged, not discouraged. The damaging aspects of campus politics reside not in the advocacy of opposing points of view by faculty members but in the commonplace incompetence with which such advocacy is pursued and the absence of the kind of ground rules and restrictions that disputes in our court system are subject to.

What is really needed in colleges is the kind of in-plant training program for faculty members in parliamentary procedure and persuasion that industry routinely provides to its personnel in job related matters.

Some differences in the political processes may be noted between the departmental political scene and the college or university level politics. Institutional faculty meetings tend to become more formal simply because they are larger and more unwieldy. These meetings often tend to be dominated by a handful of the more verbose faculty members primarily because the others are too unfamiliar with proper parliamentary procedure to be able to participate effectively. Even if you do not desire to take an active role in such proceedings, you should study *Robert's Rules of Order* (or whatever other handbook your school uses as its source of procedural authority) so that if the occasion ever arises when you must get involved with an issue being debated your ignorance of the procedural mechanics involved will not prevent your participation in the discussion.

Most faculty organizations from a department on up are too large to function effectively *en masse* and consequently do the bulk of their work through committees. If you desire to have an effective role in the policies and operation of your institution then the best way to accomplish this end is to get yourself appointed to those departmental or college committees that deal with the areas of your principal interests.

University or college committees are a good way of meeting and getting known by people outside of your department, if your future plans include possible administrative positions. However, they are not just social clubs and you should not seek a committee post unless you have the time available to do the required work. The beginning faculty member would do well to limit his committee work to one or two committees until he has a better idea of just what is involved, although this can vary greatly as a function of how active the committee chairman is.

In the final analysis it is important for a professor to get involved with the governance of his department or college even if his primary interest is in teaching because these organizations provide the settings and conditions under which a teacher must operate. If these conditions are not optimally suitable for teaching, and they usually aren't, then both faculty and student standards will suffer. The fact is that universities are run by faculties to a much greater extent than by their administrative staffs, and we all bear a direct responsibility for how good or bad our institutions may be. If you do not get involved then you are responsible by default for the *status quo*.

To have an effective voice in the running of your school requires that you expend considerable time and effort to learn how it is organized and how it functions. This is as much of an obligation of a teacher to his students as is the preparation of acceptable lectures.

13.
Publish or Perish

The need for a professor to be active in publishing material in so-called scholarly journals is a real fact of academic life. The extent of a faculty member's activity in this area is probably the most important single factor in determining his professional recognition, his chances for getting promotions and tenure, and his job mobility.

The reasons given by most institutions of higher learning for this undue emphasis on publication usually boil down to the equating of publishing with scholarship. It is difficult to accept such a clearly spurious answer as indicative of the actual reason. True scholarship refers to a state of mind. It may on occasion be evidenced by literary efforts, but more often it exhibits itself in a private manner such as a lifelong preoccupation with reading, study, and reflection.

While I do not purport to understand why the equation of publications with scholarship is so widespread, I suspect that there are two reasons for this phenomenon. The fact of publication is both obvious and objective. The evaluation of teaching ability and the ability to work effectively with students is a much more difficult and time consuming matter. Hence people who must make personnel decisions concerning

faculty and potential faculty find the straightforward count-
ing of the number of publications that an applicant is responsible for a more convenient and supportable basis for decision
making. Also a list of publications can supply an objective
basis for supporting or opposing a colleague's tenure or promotion application when the real reason for the position taken on
this issue is not as socially acceptable.

Whatever the reasons may be for adopting a policy of
publish or perish, there is little uncertainty regarding the effects that this policy has had on colleges, faculty, and students.
In a nutshell the effects are to load colleges down with low
quality, poorly motivated teachers; downgrade the teaching
ability of faculty members; and assure the neglect of student
needs. These deleterious effects are produced because if a professor knows, and hopefully few are stupid enough not to
know, that his advancement and tenure opportunities depend
on his publication record much more so than on his ability
to work effectively with students, then he is motivated to neglect his teaching responsibilities and devote as much time as
possible to the bolstering of his publication credits. Why
should a professor try to improve his lectures if he knows that
he will receive little recognition for this effort? Not many
people have the character to be deaf to the voice of self-
interest, particularly if the course of conduct involved can be
cloaked in such euphemistic terms as "scholarly activity."

Not only is the educational system harmed by the overemphasis on scholarly publications but true scholarship and
research are hindered in at least two ways.

First, people doing research tend to be concerned not in
investigating problems that need investigation but in selecting
problems where the results will be easy to get published. This
results in a large number of trivial studies being performed
while at the same time it practically assures that nobody is
likely to do the necessary type of replicational studies needed
to develop confidence in previous findings because they are
difficult or impossible to get published.

Second, this deluge of garbage studies has a tendency to crowd the literature and makes it more difficult for quality work to find its way into print. It also makes it harder for a researcher to find important studies when they do get published as they are buried among the more numerous spurious papers.

It should be made clear that I am not advocating a campaign against publishing by individual college professors. Aside from the fact that as a practical matter this would be advising the reader to commit professional suicide, such an extreme position is unwarranted.

The basic need for change is in the attitudes of universities. These institutions must begin to realize that publications are only one of the many ways in which scholarship is reflected. They also need a more realistic values system wherein ability to work effectively with classes and individual students is assigned a higher priority than it now enjoys. If universities begin to think realistically about what faculty skills are really the most important to these institutions, instead of thinking in terms of platitudes and impressive sounding but meaningless statements of principles, they may yet find within themselves the means of their salvation.

Whatever the proper amount of relative weight that should be accorded to faculty publications, more attention to quality than to quantity is in order. Perhaps if the writing of a low quality or trivial paper or the stealing of a student paper by the instructor's adding his name to it counted against rather than in favor of a professor, the quality of the literature would be upgraded with surprising rapidity and the publication lag reduced significantly.

I vividly remember a graduate engineering student telling me with some pride that he had now reached that stage of professional development where he was able to understand 50 percent of the articles in a certain engineering journal. It is hard to think of a more severe indictment of that publication or the motivation of its authors.

This story illustrates the practice of making journal articles complicated and incorporating as much esoteric terminology and mathematical formulae in them as possible because their purpose is often not to inform the reader but to enhance the prestige of the writer. One is also tempted to speculate how often the real purpose behind this writing style is to induce the editor to publish the material by making him reluctant to admit that he doesn't understand all of the profound concepts contained in it. For some time I have been considering submitting an article to a space journal entitled "A Spectrographic Analysis of Lunar Content" which would set forth in complicated and mathematical terms the proposition that the moon is made of Swiss cheese. I would then cover all bets that the article would be published and that nobody would notice its meaning. The real impediment to this project is the firm conviction that this article, and many like it, have already been published and gone unnoticed.

The time to consider submitting an article for publication is when two things coexist. You have something to say and you believe that it is worth saying. With confidence that the reader will restrict his efforts at publication to situations meeting this test, a few principles will be given that may facilitate the acceptance of material submitted for publication.

The most important single factor in getting a study published is to submit it to the proper journal. Professional journals vary widely in the type of material that they will publish and knowing which ones to submit a proposed paper to can save a lot of wasted time and effort. Often the journals themselves will have a section devoted to advising readers as to what types of articles they seek for publication and the manner in which and to whom they should be submitted. Colleagues will be another useful source of information with respect to the proper journal for an article, as will be your own familiarity with the type of material published in the periodicals that you regularly review.

With all of the emphasis on publishing by universities,

it is odd that they do not all have an office whose sole full-time task is to place the articles of faculty and staff with the proper journal, thereby freeing the professorial staff of this mechanical and time consuming effort, especially since a specialist could probably do much to reduce the publication lag of a particular study by submitting it to the journal most likely to accept it in the first instance.

A second important consideration is that the article must be prepared in the format that the publisher requires, if the editor is not to be distracted from its content by its form. In most professions there are common standards for many individual journals as typified by the American Psychological Association's *Publication Manual,* but individual journals may have minor idiosyncracies of their own and these should be investigated and conformed to before submitting a paper to them, even if this necessitates rewriting portions of a paper.

Papers should be submitted to only one journal at a time and this can produce a substantial publication lag if the journals you submit material to take a protracted period of time to accept or reject a paper. This delay is not always the journal's fault as they are often swamped with papers to review submitted by faculty seeking fame and promotion, but after a reasonable period of time you can inquire as to when you can expect a decision. If a particular journal has a long time interval between the submission of a paper and the rendering of a decision about it, you might bear this in mind when deciding which journals to submit future papers to. However, the reputation of the periodical and its appropriateness for the paper are the most important factors to consider.

Since there is such a deluge of material submitted for publication and since page space is expensive and at a premium it follows that a short, succinct paper covering the material as adequately as a more verbose one stands a much better chance of being accepted. It is a rare paper indeed that can't be shortened substantially without altering its informational content by the elimination of redundancies and the judicious replacement of needlessly long phrases with the appropriate choice of a one- or two-word substitute.

If the essence of a three hundred page doctoral thesis can be captured in a one hundred and twenty-five word abstract there is rarely an excuse for the final draft of a paper to be much longer than about one-half of the first draft.

In addition to being concise, if the paper is well written from a grammatical and stylistic point of view it will be a great help. Breakfast cereal manufacturers spend millions of dollars to package their products attractively because they know how important it is. Your writing style is the packaging that you use to transmit your ideas in and it can go a long way, not just in making these ideas attractive to a publisher but even more importantly, in clarifying them for your ultimate professional audience. This doesn't mean that you have to be able to write like a Hemingway or a Fitzgerald, but it does mean that you should review your sentence structure and style to eliminate ambiguities of meaning. Science has been described as a rough game and the ideas set forth in professional papers are often subject to scathing attacks, particularly if they offend the pet theories of others. If your writing gets such a reaction at least it should be elicited by what you intended to say and not by a misunderstanding of your meaning which was encouraged by the awkward or ambiguous way in which your ideas were expressed.

Lest the reader be frightened by the prospect of creating controversy he should know that the most common reaction to a paper is a couple of dozen requests for reprints, which are quite flattering, followed by oblivion, interrupted periodically by an occasional request for a reprint by some graduate student who has stumbled across the article while reviewing the literature for his course work. Incidentally, requests for reprints tend to follow the distribution of the journals and can be a stamp collector's delight.

The last important point to bear in mind in getting a paper published is the need for persistence. It doesn't pay to get dejected when your prize paper is rejected, but it is important to consider carefully the reasons given for the rejection. Often it will have nothing to do with the merits of your work but simply be the result of your having made the wrong choice of a journal. If the paper is rejected for cause, often the rejection will contain sound reasons and these may suggest a way to improve the paper and make it more acceptable to the same or another publisher. Sometimes an article will be rejected because of the editor's lack of understanding of the subject matter. I remember being upset on one occasion when an article of mine on the subject of stereotypes was rejected with a notation that it contributed nothing new to the understanding of attitudes!

If you get a rejection notice and the reasons given for the rejection reflect a lack of understanding of the subject matter of your paper by the editor it is nothing to get discouraged about, but if this situation occurs frequently with papers that you prepare or several times with the same one it might be a good idea to ask a colleague or two to read it to be sure that the problem is with the ineptitude of the editors in question and not with the confusing or obtuse quality of your prose.

In the case of a book as opposed to an article or journal paper it is a good plan not to write it until you have a contract for its publication because of the much greater amount of time, money, and effort that will have to be invested in such an undertaking. Unlike the situation with a paper, in the case of a proposed book it is proper and necessary to submit your proposal to many publishers simultaneously.

If several publishers offer you a contract for the book your choice will involve consideration not just of the amount of any advance or the percentage rates of royalties but the amount of marketing effort that the publisher will make and the quality of production. It is possible to get a greater return on a book at a lower royalty rate if it is placed with a publisher who exploits it more actively.

If only one publisher offers you a contract the only decision you have to make is whether the probable compensation both direct (in the form of money) and indirect (in the form of professional advancement) is worth the amount of work involved. You should never sign a contract with any publisher that you are unfamiliar with without looking him up in trade journals and inspecting samples of his books to insure that you are dealing with a reputable firm. You don't want to be in the position of being embarrassed to have your name appear on a low quality production job or work for a year or two on a book that will not be published because the publisher has gone out of business.

After you submit a proposal to thirty or forty publishers and get no offers of a contract, you know there probably is not too much of a market for the work you are proposing and you might be well advised to abandon the project unless you feel strongly about it, in which case don't give up until you run out of publishers.

There are some publishing firms called vanity houses in the trade that will publish a book at the author's expense. Paying to publish your own book is a mistake because you will generally not have the marketing facilities to properly exploit a book so published. This marketing organization is the real value of a publisher to an author. What is needed is a publisher motivated to market your book as a result of the investment he has made in its production. A visit to any bookstore should convince the reader that it is possible for him to find a publisher for a book on almost anything if he looks hard enough.

To propose a book to a publisher it is necessary to provide him with some basis on which to make a decision that the book will or will not prove profitable for him to produce. The usual materials submitted to provide this basis for a decision will be a tentative outline of the book in enough detail to give the publisher a reasonable idea of exactly what it is that you are proposing to do, a sample chapter or two to give some indication of your writing style and a professional resumé setting forth your qualifications to produce a work on the subject selected.

Book rejections sent to college professors do not tend to

be as informative as paper rejections do as they are sent by the same book companies that depend on college professors to specify their products and hence they are anxious to avoid giving offense.

In general they will say something to the effect that the entire editorial staff threatened to resign if the managing editor refused your book, but unfortunately he had to do so, in spite of the great personal pain it caused him, because of previous commitments. These are probably the only rejection letters you will ever get that actually lift your spirits even if they won't help much in the improvement of your proposal.

Occasionally an editor will tell you that he is interested in your book but that he wants to see the finished work before he is willing to make a commitment. Such an "offer" really commits neither party to anything. If the proposed book is to be more than a twenty page pamphlet, it should not be written without a firm commitment for its publication unless there are special circumstances, such as the author's planning to complete the work on a sabbatical taken for that purpose, there being no other way to work it into his schedule, or perhaps a period of convalescence provides an unusual opportunity to accomplish the often postponed task.

Since this is a book by, for, and about college teachers, it would be appropriate to end this chapter by paraphrasing a statement made by a former professor of mine many semesters ago. This gentleman advised his class that since there were too many books in the world to read in a single lifetime one should never waste his time by reading a book that wasn't worth reading. The fact that the professor in question followed this good advice with the assignment of a half-dozen texts that weren't worth reading doesn't detract from its basic soundness.

To go one step further it might be said that since there isn't enough time in life to write everything that you might like to, never waste time writing a paper or book that isn't worth reading. Nobody will.

14.
The Current Crisis in Higher Education

A generation ago the average IQ of a college graduate was found to be about 120. Present studies typically yield a value closer to 115, and it is probable that the results will be substantially lower in the future. If people with lower intellectual ability are now able to successfully complete a course of college level studies when formerly they were unable to do so, it follows that academic standards must have eroded over the years. Actually the term "eroded" is a poor choice of a word as it implies a slow process, while in fact academic standards have fallen at an alarming rate.

There have been many pressures in recent years that have tended to produce the reduction of academic standards. One of the strongest of these is the American fiction that college is for everyone and that it is necessary to assure eligibility for the better job opportunities.

The idea that everyone is entitled to a college education results from misapplying the sound democratic political principle that every person should be equal before the law to an area where it has no legitimate application. We may all be born equal with respect to political rights, at least in theory, but we are certainly not all born equal with respect to intel-

lectual ability. If everyone is required to have a college education because of social pressure, and if the IQ of the average
person is 100, then it follows that college level work must be
downgraded to a level that can be handled successfully by a
person with an IQ well below 100. The question must then
be asked, what is to be done for the students who are capable
of doing college level work and who will be needed to meet
the country's requirements for the next generation of doctors,
engineers, lawyers, teachers, and other professionals? Will a
Ph.D. ultimately become the equivalent of a former bachelor's
degree and will some new type of super doctorate have to
be created?

Maybe what is necessary is to replace the ads on television
urging teenagers not to drop out of school with ads directed at
a more selective audience. The best advice that could be given
to some students would be to drop out of a program that they
are unsuited for and to find some type of work from which
they are capable of attaining some degree of success and
fulfillment.

To profit from a college experience a student needs more
than just intellectual ability. He must have both the emotional stability and the motivation to profit from college
work. Education is much like psychotherapy in that a student
can't be forced into it by parental pressure. To be successful
the student himself has to want to be in school. This readi-
ness for higher education does not automatically occur upon
graduation from high school and many students would profit
from a year or two of work experience prior to entering college. The well-known phenomenon of the late bloomer who
does poorly in his early years in college but who finally
emerges as a first rate student is probably due to such a student's being forced to start college before he was ready.

There is another important advantage to be gained by a
student from prior work experience and that is the opportunity to be able to contribute to the payment of his expenses
at college. It may sound as if this is more of an advantage to

his parents than to himself but actually the reverse is true. In order to get the most out of his college education the student must value it and the simple fact is that we do not value things that are gotten for nothing as much as we do those that we must pay a price for. It is a well-known phenomenon among lawyers that if free professional advice is given to a friend the most likely reaction is the friend's assertion that the advice is all wrong. A client charged $50 for the same advice will never disparage it.

The notion that a liberal arts education is some type of job training probably resulted from the fact that when academic standards were higher the attaining of a college degree was indicative of some minimal amount of intellectual ability, maturity, and persistence. Hopefully as the possession of a degree assures less and less of these qualities, employment managers will come to realize that such attributes are not the exclusive possession of college graduates, and this may ultimately lower the pressure on teenagers to attend college solely to enhance their competitive position in the job market.

Closely related to the idea of the universal desirability of a college education is the awakening of society to the restricted educational opportunities of certain ethnic minority groups. This has led to further pressures to reduce academic standards to enable students who have been deprived of a quality education in grammar or high school to nevertheless get a college diploma and go out and compete in the job market on an equal basis with others.

While the problems of educationally deprived minority students must be recognized and dealt with effectively, the idea that these problems can be solved by issuing such students watered down, meaningless diplomas is simplistic in the extreme. It rests on the assumption that somehow the colleges are either responsible for social injustice and must therefore be required to rectify it or that they at least have it in their power to do so. Neither assumption is correct.

What disadvantaged students need is neither a worthless

degree nor the opportunity to enter into and flunk out of a real college level program but instead some precollege remedial program which will enable them to enter college and to compete on a realistic basis with other students. Such a program is more expensive and time-consuming than the lowering of existing academic standards and is hence politically less popular, but if the needs of minority communities for professional people are to be met by supplying them with a collection of poorly trained doctors and lawyers who were given their degrees on the basis of society's feelings of guilt rather than on the basis of demonstrated professional ability, it will prove a far greater outrage than has ever been perpetrated on them in the past.

As the middle-class American preoccupation with education as a status symbol grew it became politically expedient for the states to expand their public school systems into the area of college education. Instead of providing subsidies to permit students to attend the college of their choice and thus permit these institutions to improve their faculty salary structures, enabling them to improve the caliber of their staffs, the states generally have elected to waste available funds by building redundant physical facilities and competing with the private colleges. Since private colleges, with the exception of a few still able to live off their former reputations, are unable to compete with a state system charging less than half of the tuition for the same courses, many private institutions have been driven to the point of bankruptcy and are forced to lower admission standards in the attempt to remain open.

An example of the extremes that colleges have been driven to by public competition can be seen in recent offers by some colleges to give up to two years of college credit for "life experience." This is really nothing more or less than a promotional gimmick designed to increase enrollment by awarding a four-year college diploma for the cut-rate price of two years of work and tuition. If this trend continues it may be possible in the foreseeable future to get a master's degree in criminology by going to jail for a year or two.

There is an even more ominous consideration attending a state's entry into the field of higher education. Eventually as competition from low tuition state schools forces private colleges to go out of business the state will either have to provide subsidies to private college students or take over these institutions to provide an education for the students whose school it has destroyed. If it takes the latter course the state must ultimately end up with exclusive control over all higher education. In view of the recent Watergate debacle it should be quite obvious that if there is any situation more dangerous to a free people than a government's control of the press then it almost certainly must be a government's control over all of the instrumentalities of higher education.

The founding fathers of this country clearly recognized the essential antagonism between any form of government and human liberties, especially the freedom of speech and expression that is necessary to education and science. This is why the Bill of Rights was enacted to protect individual citizens against the feared excesses of governmental action.

The complete or even substantial control over education by any government is a potential threat to individual liberties that dwarfs by comparison any of the dangers posed by foreign enemies that we have become so expensively preoccupied with in recent years.

During the 1960s another attack was made against the integrity of a college degree, but this time the threat was of a noneconomic nature. Student activists launched a multifront attack on the war in Vietnam, current social values, the establishment in general, and on many phases of academic life.

Many of the students' complaints were justifiable, some weren't, but the tactics of rebellious students such as the taking over of campus buildings or disrupting classes turned many universities into a state of chaos. Had these situations been properly handled there would have been no problem. Student leaders could have been told where the line of acceptable behavior was drawn, and within reasonable limits (set to respect the rights of other students), they could have demonstrated as much as they pleased, because the vigorous expression of dissent is to be encouraged in a democracy. On the other hand if they exceeded reasonable limits of protest and took over buildings or destroyed property they could have been warned and if they persisted in such conduct, expelled.

Unfortunately most college administrators are not selected on the basis of their cool in a crisis nor on the strength of their backbones, and many of them panicked. A few overreacted but most simply knuckled under to almost any student demand, hoping that such capitulation would somehow keep the peace. The predictable effect of this reinforcement of student disruption was of course more student disruption and demands. There were times when student strike leaders were hard put to think of what to ask for next. Courses were all taken on a pass/fail basis and final exams were omitted. Course requirements were dropped. In some institutions it became possible to get a degree without ever having to take a required course. We are still living with the effects of many of these mindless concessions to unreasonable student demands and they will continue to damage future students for years to come.

The idea of there being no required sequence of courses in a degree program implies that the student is competent to determine what ideas he should be exposed to even though he is ignorant of the potentialities involved. If a student is really competent to decide on what courses he needs to attain his specific educational goals then he is wasting his time and money in college. Many of the students who quit courses midway through them in reliance on a meaningless grade of P have subsequently paid a price in the form of graduate school rejections, but few professors took the trouble to warn them of this risk in the turmoil of the times.

All of the factors mentioned heretofore have contributed to what is the major crisis in higher education today: the cheapening of a college degree and the proliferation of an excessive amount of cheap degrees from the bachelor's level on up to the doctorate, accompanied by a paucity of qualified graduates at any level.

The real challenge that must be met by the colleges is to reverse this trend and preserve the integrity of a college degree. While the capitulation under pressure of the colleges to ill-advised student demands has been generally harmful, it must be recognized that there are many aspects of a college experience that are inefficient or counterproductive and these defects urgently require correction.

For example, a college education often takes longer than is necessary. As the technology explosion continues, it is likely that there will be a greater need in the future for people trained in more than one discipline. This situation already exists in many fields such as a patent attorney who must be both a lawyer and an engineer, or a human factors specialist who must combine engineering training with preparation in psychology. The situation can be anticipated where a particular job may require a person trained in three or four different fields. If it takes from four to eight years of training to be prepared in each constituent field such a specialist, produced at a staggering training cost, may have only the briefest of professional lives before he is ready to retire unless the training process can be significantly reduced.

If a reduction in the length of a college education is not to adversely affect its quality then what must be eliminated are redundancies and inefficiencies, not the number of new ideas that the student is exposed to. For example, there is often a great deal of overlap between basic college courses in physics, chemistry, or biology and the courses in the same areas that the students have taken in high school. Some students may require this review; most don't. Why not offer these basic courses in one- and two-semester sections, the latter for students with no prior work in the area and the former for students who studied the course in high school and need to build from an established base of knowledge, not repeat the course *ab initio*?

Much of the reason for the unduly long time it takes to complete college is due to administrative convenience. For example, the average college course is three semester hours in duration and the instructor will expose his class to three semester hours' worth of material regardless of whether an adequate coverage of the course content requires twenty semester hours or if it could be properly treated in two or three class meetings. Similarly, it arbitrarily takes four years of full time study to get a bachelor's degree without regard to the nature of the field in which a student majors. In some professional areas such as engineering there is an enormous amount of material to be mastered and it might be justifiable to require five or more years to attain a first degree in these areas, while in other fields three years may be excessive. In a liberal arts program where students are not being trained for professional work in their majors an arbitrary period of exposure to new ideas must necessarily be set, but if the material can be packaged more efficiently this period can be utilized more effectively.

There is a move afoot to reduce the amount of time spent in some medical schools from four to three years in response to the shortage of doctors and the enormous expense of a medical education. If this reduction in time is accompanied by an improvement in efficiency so that standards of training are maintained or improved it will be a step in the right direction. Another partial solution to this problem might be to conduct medical schools on a three shift basis so that expensive laboratory facilities and equipment can be utilized on an around the clock basis.

Perhaps the ultimate solution will lie in the states' de-emphasizing competition with undergraduate institutions where it is harmful and emphasizing competition with graduate and professional schools where it would be useful under present conditions.

There is a limit to the amount of time compression that is desirable in education which is imposed by the essential nature of the process. Students need a certain amount of time to mull over and digest new concepts.

The danger in the overemphasis on the mechanical aspects of improving educational efficiency is that the needs and limitations of the individual student may be overlooked. Nothing could prove more disastrous, for the entire complex and costly educational machinery exists for no other legitimate purpose than to serve student needs.

Until the time arrives when there are adequate training facilities for all qualified graduate and professional students, better criteria for their selection are required, to assure that the best potential practitioners are admitted. These in general will not prove to be the people selected solely on the basis of their likelihood to pass all of the coursework.

It might be suggested, somewhat facetiously, as a solution to the problem of colleges being filled with students who do not want to be there or who don't belong there but who are forced to attend by social, family, or vocational pressures that a degree be immediately issued to all students on the basis of their paying a fee equal to four years' tuition. At the time of the conferring of this degree the person would also be given the option of attending lectures for the next four years if he so desires. Such an arrangement might help end the preoccupation with degrees which has been the major cause of the problems of most colleges and permit colleges to resume their proper function of servicing students interested in getting an education.

Another possible change in the educational system which is equally unlikely to be adopted, but which would do much to improve the quality of teaching, would be to enable college professors to go into private practice as teachers. Thus instead of working for an institution the teacher would be licensed in the fields of his competency and he would hire a lecture hall, give individual courses and award certificates of completion to his students, who, when they had collected enough such certificates from different professors, could turn them in to the state in exchange for a diploma. Obviously such an arrangement would deprive students of many services currently rendered to them by colleges, such as guidance, counseling, and dormitories, but it would have one overwhelming advantage. Good teachers would prosper and poor ones would be driven from the profession. Perhaps this same desirable result could be obtained if the colleges paid a professor a percentage of the tuition brought in by his courses instead of a fixed salary.

Lest the emphasis on the problems confronting college education, both financial and educational, leave the reader depressed, it must be said that there is little doubt that the colleges will survive even though it will probably be in some substantially altered and hopefully improved form. They will survive for the simple reason that they are essential to provide the next generation of scientists and leaders for the country.

The reader may take heart in the realization of how dull it would be to work in a profession where there were no such momentous problems requiring solutions.

Appendix

FIGURE 1

NAME: _____
Address: _____

Approved for Graduation _____

Not approved _____

By: _____

UNIVERSITY REQUIREMENTS:

Cum Average 2.00
Semester hrs. 124
Liberal Arts 94

	Sem.	Grade
English 1 (3)		
English 2 (3)		

HUMANITIES (6)
(Drama, English, Fine Arts, Humanities 1-2, Music)

SOCIAL SCIENCES (6)
(Anthropology, Economics, Geography, History, Political Science, Sociology, Soc. Sc.)

PSYCHOLOGY REQUIREMENTS* (30 s.h.)

	Sem.	Grade
*Psy 1 (3)		
*Psy 2 (3)		
*Psy 140 (4)—Measurement & Statistics		
*Psy 141 (4)—Research Method & Design (Prereq. to all 190 courses)		

*RESEARCH SEMINAR (4 s.h.)

Psy 190, 191—in Experimental Psy. Prereq: 140 and 141

Psy 192, 193—in Operant Behavior Prereq: 140 and 141

Psy 194, 195—in Physiological Psy. Prereq: 141 and 177

Psy 196, 197—in Developmental Psy. Prereq: 141 and 153 or 154

Psy 198, 199—in Social Psy. Prereq: 141 and 159

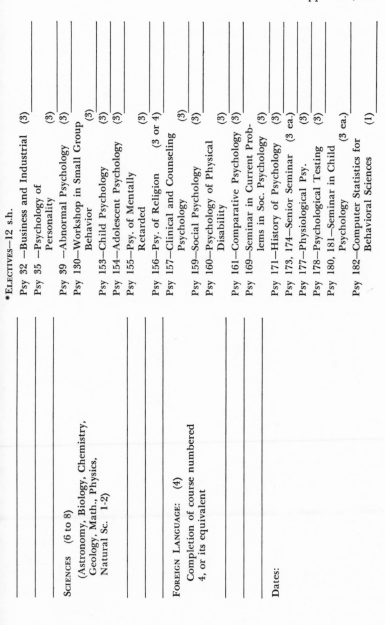

*Electives—12 s.h.

Psy 32 —Business and Industrial	(3)
Psy 35 —Psychology of Personality	(3)
Psy 39 —Abnormal Psychology	(3)
Psy 130—Workshop in Small Group Behavior	(3)
Psy 153—Child Psychology	(3)
Psy 154—Adolescent Psychology	(3)
Psy 155—Psy. of Mentally Retarded	(3)
Psy 156—Psy. of Religion	(3 or 4)
Psy 157—Clinical and Counseling Psychology	(3)
Psy 159—Social Psychology	(3)
Psy 160—Psychology of Physical Disability	(3)
Psy 161—Comparative Psychology	(3)
Psy 169—Seminar in Current Problems in Soc. Psychology	(3)
Psy 171—History of Psychology	(3)
Psy 173, 174—Senior Seminar	(3 ea.)
Psy 177—Physiological Psy.	(3)
Psy 178—Psychological Testing	(3)
Psy 180, 181—Seminar in Child Psychology	(3 ea.)
Psy 182—Computer Statistics for Behavioral Sciences	(1)

Sciences   (6 to 8)

(Astronomy, Biology, Chemistry, Geology, Math., Physics, Natural Sc. 1-2)

Foreign Language: (4)

Completion of course numbered 4, or its equivalent

Dates:

FIGURE 2

DEPARTMENT OF PSYCHOLOGY
Hofstra University
Hempstead, New York

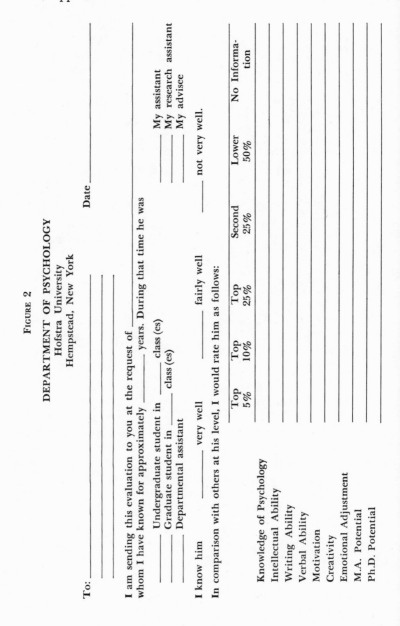

To: _____   Date _____

I am sending this evaluation to you at the request of _____
whom I have known for approximately _____ years. During that time he was

_____ Undergraduate student in _____ class (es)   _____ My assistant
_____ Graduate student in _____ class (es)   _____ My research assistant
_____ Departmental assistant   _____ My advisee

I know him _____ very well   _____ fairly well   _____ not very well.

In comparison with others at his level, I would rate him as follows:

	Top 5%	Top 10%	Top 25%	Second 25%	Lower 50%	No Information
Knowledge of Psychology						
Intellectual Ability						
Writing Ability						
Verbal Ability						
Motivation						
Creativity						
Emotional Adjustment						
M.A. Potential						
Ph.D. Potential						

I feel that his grades do (do not) represent his level of ability.

In summary, I would give him a

_____ Very strong recommendation

_____ Strong recommendation

_____ Average recommendation

_____ Recommendation with reservation

_____ No recommendation

Comments _____

_____

_____

Signature _____

Title _____

FIGURE 3

Course Number _____ Hour _____ Instructor _____
Here is a list of questions concerning your feelings about the course and the
instructor. Answer each question by circling the number which corresponds
to your judgment. The extremes represented by Numbers 1 and 7 are defined for you within each question. You may use any one of the numbers
listed. Think carefully before making your rating.

1.	Presentation of subject matter 1—clear and well organized 7—unclear and disorganized	1 2 3 4 5 6 7
2.	Class time 1—always entertaining 7—always dull	1 2 3 4 5 6 7
3.	Class participation 1—all the time 7—never	1 2 3 4 5 6 7
4.	Teacher's personality in the classroom 1—always pleasant 7—always unpleasant	1 2 3 4 5 6 7
5.	Fairness in grading 1—too hard 7—too easy	1 2 3 4 5 6 7
6.	Opinions of the papers 1—too many 7—too few	1 2 3 4 5 6 7
7.	Opinions of the test questions 1—very clear 7—unclear	1 2 3 4 5 6 7
8.	Quality of the teaching 1—excellent 7—poor	1 2 3 4 5 6 7
9.	How much did you learn from the text? 1—a great deal 7—nothing	1 2 3 4 5 6 7
10.	How much did you learn from the lecture? 1—a great deal 7—nothing	1 2 3 4 5 6 7
11.	How much did you learn from the course as a whole? 1—a great deal 7—nothing	1 2 3 4 5 6 7
12.	Did this course affect your interest in the subject matter? 1—increased my interest 7—decreased my interest	1 2 3 4 5 6 7

(ON THE REVERSE SIDE WRITE ANY COMMENTS
YOU HAVE ABOUT THE COURSE.)

FIGURE 4

Course _____ Instructor _____ Date _____

Please assign a grade to each aspect of the course listed below. In grading, compare this course with other courses you have taken. Grade meanings are as follows:

> A=Excellent
> B=Better than average
> C=Average
> D=Below average
> F=Inferior

Then, give your reasons for each grade in the space provided. List what you liked and/or disliked as explicitly as possible. If you need more room, write on the back of this sheet.

1._____Instructor's command of the subject matter.

2._____Instructor's enthusiasm for subject matter.

3._____Instructor's explanation of subject matter.

4._____Instructor's personality in classroom.

5._____Instructor's assistance outside classroom.

6._____Amount you learned in course.

7._____Quality of textbook.

8._____Quality of assignments.

9._____Overall rating of course.

10. Additional comments:

Index

About the Author

This guide represents the practical know-how acquired by Roy Udolf through a decade of teaching experience as well as a lifetime of involvement with teachers and colleges. He was educated at New York University College of Engineering (B.E.E.), Brooklyn Law School (LL.B., J.D.), Hofstra University (M.A.), and Adelphi University (Ph.D.). He is a clinical psychologist, a lawyer, an engineer, and, at present, an assistant professor of psychology at Hofstra University. His past experience includes twenty years of engineering and management related to complex electronic controls in navigational and communication systems. He has also practiced criminal law for two years.

Dr. Udolf has contributed to numerous professional, technical, and scholarly publications and is the author of a book published in 1974 by Nelson-Hall, *Logic Design for Behavioral Scientists*. The professional societies in which he holds membership include the American Institute of Aeronautics and Astronautics, the American Psychology-Law Society, the New York State Bar Association, and the American Psychological Association.